KS3 Science

Homework Book 3

Collins

GW00778140

Graham Farrall

William Collins's dream of knowledge for all began with the publication of his first book in 1819. A self-educated mill worker, he not only enriched millions of lives, but also founded a flourishing publishing house. Today, staying true to this spirit, Collins books are packed with inspiration, innovation and practical expertise. They place you at the centre of a world of possibility and give you exactly what you need to explore it.

Collins. Freedom to teach.
Published by Collins
An imprint of HarperCollinsPublishers
77-85 Fulham Palace Road
Hammersmith
London
W6 8JB

Browse the complete Collins catalogue at
www.collinseducation.com

© HarperCollinsPublishers Limited 2009

10 9 8 7 6 5 4 3 2

ISBN-13 978-0-00-730605-3

British Library Cataloguing in Publication Data. A Catalogue record for this publication is available from the British Library.

Commissioned by Penny Fowler
Project management by Alexandra Riley
Edited by Anita Clark
Proof read by Camilla Behrens
Original concept design by Jordan Publishing Design
Page layout and cover design by eMC Design Ltd, www.emcdesign.org.uk

Production by Leonie Kellman
Illustrations by Jerry Fowler, Peters & Zabransky

Printed and bound by Printing Express, Hong Kong

Contents

Introduction

Welcome to Collins KS3 Science!

Exciting homework for every Pupil Book spread

The Homework Book contains three exciting and levelled activities for every spread in the Pupil Book. There are three styles of question – test yourself, creative and digital – so that learning science is engaging and fun.

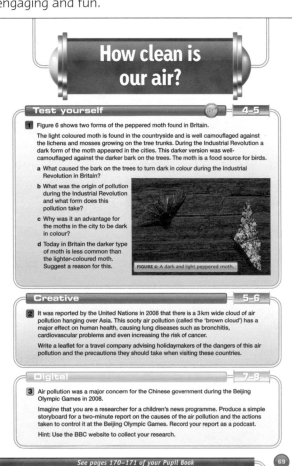

Test yourself

Test your knowledge of a topic with comprehensive test yourself questions. At the back of the book you are able to check your answers or, if you don't want to, you can tear them out at the start of your course. These questions will give you extra practice, helping you to succeed in school tests at KS3 and to prepare for GCSE.

Creative

Do you want to be a journalist for a day? How about running an advertising campaign? Or how about designing a colourful poster for your classroom?

With creative questions you can really put your science knowledge to the test with a full range of engaging activities making science fun.

Digital

Put your scientific skills to the test with our digital homeworks covering everything from creating PowerPoint presentations to making podcasts and writing wikis to share with your entire class.

If you need help on how to make a podcast or how to set up a wiki there is advice for students and teachers on our website www.collinseducation.com/ks3science

How Science Works

Look out for our HSW icons throughout the Homework Book. This is where you will really show How Science Works in your homework.

GEOLOGY PROJECT

FIGURE 1: The fossil of a small dinosaur.

The Fossil Story

Fossils give us the opportunity to study prehistoric animals and plants, and also provide us with a window of opportunity to view the habitat and climate at that time.

Imagine that you are one of a team of palaeontologists studying the fossil in Figure 1. You must use the findings from your work to create a new display for the Natural History Museum.

Use the Internet to research fossil digs, where dinosaur fossils have been found and the types of rocks in which they have been found.

Recording and interpreting your findings

Create a field notebook to record your findings. You may wish to include:

- details of the location of the site
- details of the type of rock in which the fossil was found
- any conclusions you can draw from information about the rock (for example, igneous rock may provide evidence of a volcanic eruption)
- clues provided by fossilised plant remains
- evidence of the grisly death of the dinosaur
- how the dinosaur remains have been preserved.

FIGURE 2: What would the prehistoric environment of the dinosaurs have looked like?

Modelling your findings

Create a poster for the museum display to describe the life of the animal, its habitat and sources of food. Make your description exciting and full of scientific facts.

If you have time make a model of your animal fossil for show-and-tell at the museum. (You may wish to use Plaster of Paris, clay or Plasticine.)

Health and Safety: If using Plaster of Paris, do not use your hands to make the fossil shape when the plaster is setting. The chemical process releases heat and will cause severe burns.

Explaining your findings

Create a poster for the section of the display called 'The Wider Context'. You could consider the rock cycle, how different types of rocks are formed and how landscapes change.

Hint: Use the Internet and Science books to help you to explain the wider context.

See pages 188–203 of your Pupil Book

77

Mid-Topic Projects

About half way through the topic you get a chance to see how much you've learned already by working on a project in groups in class and also at home. Science is put into context as you learn how science relates to the everyday world and has an impact on us all.

Free teaching notes for every mid-topic project are available at www.collinseducation.com/ks3science

Record your progress

At the back of this book you will see your student progress cards. All of the homeworks are levelled into levels 4–5, 5–6 and 7–8. As you work through the book, mark which homeworks you are completing for each lesson. As you move through your Key Stage 3 course you will be able to track your progress throughout each topic.

Student Progress Card	Name:		
Organisms, Behaviour and Health	4-5	5-6	7-8
Drugs and Behaviour			
What is a drug?			
Is alcohol really that good?			
A nail in the coffin			
Another nail in the coffin			
Cannabis			
Just say no			
Detecting your environment			
Being in control			
What are we born with?			
Learning behaviour in animals			
Aggression			
How do I learn?			
Effective learning			
Variation			

What is a drug?

1 **a** Use Excel to copy and complete the following crossword for an article in the school newspaper entitled 'What is a drug?'. A start has been made for you – now complete the 'across' and 'down' clues and use these to fill in the crossword.

Across	Down
1 Drug taken by clubbers	1 Increases brain activity
2	2 Slows down the nervous system
3	3
4	4
5	

b Pair up with a classmate and exchange your crosswords by e-mail. You must both have your completed crosswords ready for next lesson.

Crossword grid:
- 2 across: edicine (medicine)
- 3 across: addit (addict)
- 4 down: brai (brain)
- 4 across: endorphins
- 5 across: ablet (tablet)
- b down

2 **a** Copy and complete the sentences using the words below:

     caffeine   stimulants   symptoms   chemicals
     depressants   tranquillisers   heroin

Drugs are .... that alter the way in which your body behaves. Cocaine and .... are .... that increase brain activity, whilst .... such as .... and .... slow down the nervous system. If addicts try to stop taking a drug they will suffer from withdrawal .... such as anxiety.

b Why is it dangerous to drive under the influence of drugs?

c Explain the reason why many people prefer to drink caffeine-free cola drinks and coffee before they retire to bed.

d Explain why a large proportion of burglaries and mugging crimes are drug-related.

3 Leah Betts was a young schoolgirl who tragically died after taking one ecstasy tablet.

Prepare a speech to be given as part of an anti-drugs conference. Your speech must point out the dangers of drugs and express how Leah's parents would have felt as a result of their daughter's death. Make sure that your speech is factual and not just an expression of your own opinions.

Is alcohol really that good?

Test yourself

1 This graph shows how alcohol affects speeding when driving.

a What trend does the graph show between speeding drivers and the time of day?

b What is the percentage change in speeding between 9 p.m.–midnight, and midnight–3 a.m.?

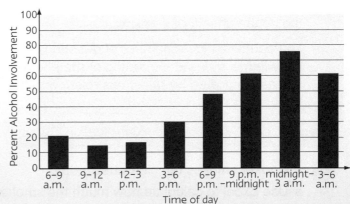

c Why do the maximum incidences of speeding occur between midnight and 3 a.m.?

d Suggest why there are more incidences of speeding between 6 a.m.–9 a.m., and 9 p.m.–midnight.

e Why are there more cases of speeding than not speeding at all times of the day when alcohol is involved?

Creative

2 The government is advocating that alcohol carries health warnings on the product labels similar to those seen on cigarette packets. Design a health warning label for an alcoholic drink. It is important that the label is illustrated, carries an important scientific fact and displays information on the units of alcohol contained in the drink.

Next, give your own arguments for or against alcohol being made illegal.

Digital

3 Alcohol companies have a responsibility to advise drinkers about drinking sensibly. Design a webpage for an alcohol company, advising on sensible drinking. It is important that your webpage carries important facts about alcohol as well as a high-impact message calling for restraint in consumption. Point out the potential health hazards caused by drinking more than the recommended number of units of alcohol, using www.nhs.uk to source information about blood alcohol concentration (BAC) related to alcohol consumption.

A nail in the coffin

Creative
4-5

1 Produce a survey questionnaire for your peers to assess the effectiveness of lessons on the health effects of smoking.

You could include a number of questions at the beginning of your survey to test knowledge and understanding of the effects that smoking has on health and the risks of disease, followed by questions relating to the reasons why young people begin smoking.

Digital

HSW · 5-6

2 A smoker smokes ten cigarettes a day.

a Use Excel to calculate how much the smoker spends on cigarettes:

   i per day   **ii** per week   **iii** per year   **iv** in 5 years

   v in 10 years   **vi** in 15 years   **vii** in 20 years.

b i Use Excel to draw a graph displaying the cost of cigarettes over a lifetime of smoking.

   ii On your graph highlight the key stages in the deterioration of the smoker's health and quality of life due to the effects of smoking cigarettes.

   iii Use the photograph of the cigarettes (left) to persuade your friends that the filters of the discarded cigarettes provide evidence that smoking can damage your health.

Present your work as an interactive whiteboard presentation as part of a smoking awareness campaign.

Test yourself

7-8

3 a The lungs in the photograph are damaged by a disease called emphysema. The tiny air sacs in the lungs are damaged by smoking and join together to become much larger.

   i Suggest how the disease affects the exchange of gases in the lungs.

   ii What effect will the disease have upon the sufferer's health?

b i Write out the equation for cellular respiration.

   ii Use the equation to explain why the sufferer of emphysema will be unable to climb a set of stairs without resting.

c What effect will the disease have upon the heart?

d Suggest an aid given to the sufferers of emphysema in order to alleviate the symptoms of the disease.

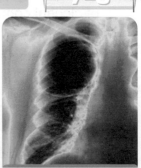

FIGURE 1: The black area shows trapped air in the lungs, caused by damage to the air sacs.

8

See pages 12–13 of your Pupil Book

Another nail in the coffin

Test yourself  **4–5**

1 The pie chart shows the percentage of deaths resulting from tobacco-related diseases.

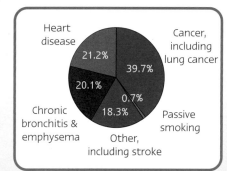

Pie chart labels: Heart disease 21.2%, Cancer, including lung cancer 39.7%, Chronic bronchitis & emphysema 20.1%, Other, including stroke 18.3%, Passive smoking 0.7%

a What is the largest cause of death from smoking?

b What is the total percentage death rate from heart and lung disease (excluding cancer) caused by smoking?

c Many smokers claim that they should have the right to smoke in public buildings. What evidence does the pie chart reveal that supports the government's ban on smoking in public buildings?

d Smokers with children place their children's health 'at risk'.

  i What is meant by the term 'at risk'?

  ii What evidence for this fact is shown in the pie chart?

Digital **5–6**

2 The smoke in cigarettes contains a mixture of gases and chemicals that gathers in the lungs of the smoker. Use the Internet to find information about the contents of cigarette smoke. Present your results as a podcast explaining the risks linked to smoking, for both smokers and people who are around smokers for long periods of time.

Creative **7–8**

3 The damage smokers do to their vascular systems means that they sometimes need organ transplants.

Cystic fibrosis is an inherited genetic disease where the person's lungs produce too much sticky mucus, causing a lifetime of illness. The disease can be fatal and some sufferers can require a lung transplant.

Case 1 – David Jones

Age:	46 years
Family:	Married with two teenage children
Occupation:	Company director in electronics industry employing 30 workers
Hobbies:	Territorial Army Officer with service in Iraq
Health:	Heavy smoker

Case 2 – Helen Johnson

Age:	14 years
Family:	Mother and father with one brother aged 18 years
Occupation:	School student
Hobbies:	Horse riding
Health:	Suffers from cystic fibrosis

Imagine that you are a member of the Hospital Trust with the burden of deciding who you would put forward for a possible lung transplant and why. Prepare your argument to persuade the panel of your important decision.

Cannabis

Digital 4-5

1 The risks linked to drink-driving are well known, but at present there is no campaign to warn drivers of the dangers of driving under the influence of cannabis.

Design an imaginative and scientifically factual webpage for a campaign warning drivers of the effects of driving and using cannabis.

Test yourself  5-6

2 This graph shows the potency (strength) of cannabis over an eight-year period.

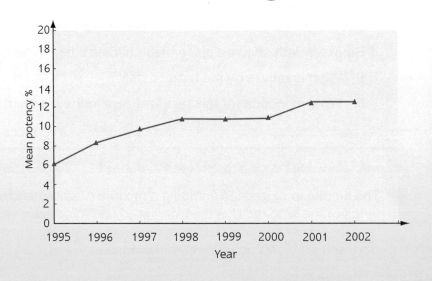

a What is the percentage change in potency of cannabis between 1995 and 2002?

b What is the trend shown in the graph?

c Why is this trend causing the authorities concern?

d What effect will the change in potency have upon the user of the drug?

e What advice should be given to the users of cannabis as a result of the changes in potency?

Creative  7-8

3 Some people who suffer from multiple sclerosis, AIDS and cancer have advocated the use of cannabis as a painkiller. Imagine that you are the judge sitting in a trial where a victim of one of these diseases is being prosecuted for illegally growing cannabis, using the drug and passing on drugs to fellow sufferers.

Write your closing speech balancing the evidence for and against the accused and delivering the jury's verdict – innocent or guilty! Ensure that your speech is a sound judgement based upon the law and scientific facts. You must also use your speech to argue whether or not you think this case demonstrates that the law should change (to become either more lenient or more severe).

Just say no

1 Imagine that you are the parent of a child who was a drug addict. Your child first tried cannabis, then moved on to a greater variety of 'hard' drugs and eventually died from an overdose. You are interviewed by the local press for a newspaper article on drug awareness. Write out your interview (including the questions asked) to reveal the effects of different drugs, the deterioration in health and destruction of a life along the timeline of your child's life, from when they first started using cannabis until their death.

Digital 5-6

2 Afghanistan's main crop is the poppy, which is used to produce heroin (the country's main export).

Use the BBC news website to research why the farmers grow the poppy. Use your findings to create a video presentation that details the devastating effects of this drug and urges the Afghanistan government to finance subsidies that will give farmers opportunities to raise their standard of living by selling food produce rather than the drug.

Test yourself 7-8

3 Study the graph opposite.

a What is the percentage difference between teenagers who took drugs and those who were offered drugs in 2004?

b What trend does the graph show in the number of drugs offered and the number of teenagers who took drugs between 1995 and 2004?

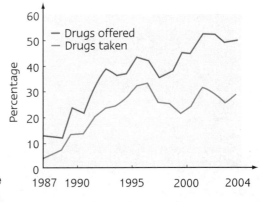

c Education about the dangers of drugs has been operating in schools in the UK. Does the graph demonstrate that this school education has been successful up to 2004?

d Ecstasy and cocaine are drugs that are associated with clubbing and partying.

   i Explain the dangers associated with these two drugs.

   ii Which do you think is most dangerous? Explain your answer.

DRUGS AND BEHAVIOUR PROJECT

The Effect of Caffeine on your Rate of Reaction

Story has it that it was the monks who first noticed that coffee stimulated them during the morning and allowed them to stay awake longer. We now know that it is the caffeine in coffee that stimulates the nervous system, improving thinking and attention.

The investigation: an introduction

Some cola drinks also contain caffeine. It is your task to investigate whether one of these drinks does indeed improve your rate of reaction.

FIGURE 2: Some drugs are legal and readily available – caffeine is easily obtained and safe to drink.

In this investigation a 30 cm ruler is dropped between the fingers and the speed of the reactions can be found by noting at which point the ruler is caught as it falls.

Carry out your investigation with friends, classmates or members of your family.

Planning your investigation

Write a plan of your investigation, considering the following points:
- how you will carry out your investigation
- what you will measure
- the range of measurements you will take
- which measurements you will repeat
- a design for your results table (including headings and units)
- how you will make your experiment a fair test (including what you will control)
- your independent and dependent variables.

Results

Use your plan to carry out your experiment. You must then bring together all your results by firstly completing your results table and then creating a graph from your results table. Use your results graph to analyse and interpret your results.

FIGURE 3: Using a ruler to test speeds of reactions.

Extend your investigation

Extend your investigation into reaction times by completing the online challenge at http://getyourwebsitehere.com/jswb/rttest01.html. Don't forget to complete the challenge twice – once without drinking a cola drink and once after drinking a cola drink.

Conclusion and evaluation

Your conclusion should describe and explain what you have found out in your planned investigation. You must then compare the results of the online reaction time tests with your results from the standard ruler investigation – how does this investigation affect the conclusion of your planned investigation?

Finally, evaluate your investigation. Comment upon the quality of your results (including suggestions for how your investigation could be improved) and explain which was the most effective way of testing your reaction times before and after drinking a cola drink.

Detecting your environment

4-5

Creative

1. Write an adventure story about your journey to school and how your nervous system saved your life on several occasions! Your story needs to explain the range of sense organs you used and how they worked to make your journey safe.

5-6

Test yourself

2. The nervous system is a complicated network of branching nerves.

   a Name the parts of the nervous system, labelled **A–C** on the diagram.

   b Which **two** parts make up the central nervous system?

   c i On the way to school James steps into the path of an oncoming car. Which sense organs will detect the potential danger?

   ii The brain will respond to the messages received from the sense organs. Produce a flow diagram detailing the nervous pathways that will protect James from the potential danger of the car.

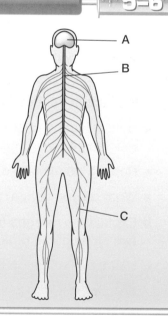

7-8

Digital

3. Diseases of the nervous system can be frightening when the victim initially lacks knowledge about the disease.

   a Use the Internet to research the effects of **two** diseases that affect the nervous system.

   b Design a webpage for NHS Direct detailing how the nervous system works and the changes that take place as a result of the disease.

See pages 22–23 of your Pupil Book

Being in control

1 a How is the brain protected?

b The brain controls functions such as body temperature. Name **two** other functions performed by the brain.

c Give **two** functions of the human brain that are special compared with the brain of other vertebrates.

d What connects the brain to the sense organs?

e Why is boxing a dangerous sport?

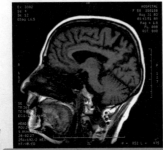

FIGURE 4: The human brain.

FIGURE 5: A sheep's brain.

2 Try this:

- Hold your hands out in front of you with the palms facing outwards.

- Cross your arms at the wrists and place your hands together, locking your fingers together.

- Now rotate your joined hands towards your body and under your chin so that they are in front of you – this is a difficult manoeuvre!

- Now ask a friend or a member of your family to point to a finger without touching it – you must respond immediately by moving only that finger.

- Repeat, pointing to different fingers.

a What do you notice?

b Explain the reasons for your unusual response and what it shows about the two sides of the brain.

c Use the information to explain the effects of having a stroke on the left-hand side of the brain.

3 Some people suffer from unusual sleep patterns and when treatments recommended by a doctor have been unproductive they may attend sleep clinics. These clinics may investigate brain waves by attaching electrodes to the brain.

Use the Internet to investigate the different alpha, beta and delta wave patterns associated with sleep. Write up your research in the way that you think would best explain the key information about brain wave patterns during sleep to patients at a sleep clinic.

What are we born with?

1 Make a funny cartoon sequence showing the role of the senses and reflexes used to protect an unlucky character from the hazards of everyday life. Add speech bubbles to your illustrations to explain the role of each sense and reflex.

2 The sense organs play an important role by informing the body about changes in the environment.

a What is the name of the action taken by the body when we touch a hot object unexpectedly?

b Identify the parts on the diagram labelled **A–D**.

c Why is part **D** important in protecting the body?

d i Name **two** actions that protect the body.

ii The brain is not directly involved in nervous responses such as these. What is the advantage of not including the brain in the nervous action?

e The frog has previously eaten a wasp only to be stung in the mouth! Explain why the frog now ignores the wasp as potential food.

3 When a baby is first born the midwife or doctor will carry out a number of reflex tests to check the baby's nervous system, including the:

stepping or walking reflex   clasp reflex   cuddle reflex   suckling reflex

Use the Internet to research a selection of these reflex actions and tests. Then explain how the newborn baby will develop learnt responses (for example, to familiar faces and voices) and how these compare with their reflex actions. Present your information as a leaflet for a maternity class to provide information for expectant mothers.

Learning behaviour in animals

1 Dogs make fantastic pets, but they can also learn to play a major role in society as, for example, dogs for the blind, sheep dogs, police dogs and search-and-rescue dogs.

Use the Internet to research the techniques used to train a dog for a specific role. Present your information on a careers website for people who wish to begin a career in dog training. Your webpage should include illustrations, a description of the role carried out by the dog, information on the age when training begins, details of the techniques and stages in progression, and an outline of the dog's final test in real-life situations.

Test yourself   5-6

2 a Link the words to the statements.

Train	to respond to a stimulus
Obey	to provide an incentive
Motivate	to instruct
Behaviour	to do what you are told

b During training, a dog is often provided with a titbit of food. What type of reinforcement is this?

c What alternative to a food titbit could a trainer use when a dog carries out a trick correctly?

d Suggest how you could train a dog to retrieve a ball.

e Suggest **two** examples of negative reinforcement when training a dog.

f What can puppies learn from watching their parents?

Creative    7-8

3 Many circuses in Britain have stopped using animals as part of their act. However, in some countries performing animals are still used to draw in the crowds.

Write a letter to the RSPCA stressing your opinions on circuses that still use performing animals. You could detail the ethics of: caging animals and restricting their movements; training animals to perform potentially dangerous and spectacular tricks in noisy arenas; the taming of wild animals; and the transportation of the animals around the country for many weeks without rest.

Aggression

1 During the 2008–09 season, the Football Association (F.A.) launched a campaign to encourage more families to attend football matches.

a Explain how the F.A. is hoping that this initiative will reduce aggressive behaviour at football matches.

b In what ways is aggressive behaviour demonstrated at a football match?

c Suggest why the F.A. has banned alcohol at football matches.

d In what way does aggressive behaviour at a football match mimic animal aggression in the wild?

FIGURE 6: Violence at a football match.

Creative 5-6

2 Aggressive behaviour fuelled by alcohol is a major concern for the police and authorities. CCTV reveals gangs of youths involved in aggressive attacks (very often involving knives).

Write an editorial article for a young persons' magazine detailing the signs and causes of aggression, and the nature of the aggression towards people who are vulnerable. As Editor-in-Chief it is your role to express your opinions about such aggressive behaviour and the effects that it has upon young people and society.

Digital 7-8

3 Dogs are pack animals and when humans have a pet dog the owner plays the role of the pack leader.

Use the Internet to research aggressive dog behaviours that are a response to the fact that their ancestors belonged to a pack in the wild. Use your research to produce a wiki for a dog training class, explaining the nature behind one of the following potentially aggressive behaviours:

defending territory   establishing dominance   self-defence

How do I learn?

1 'Kim's Game' is a memory game. Ten objects are placed on a tray and after one minute the tray is covered with a cloth. The player then recalls the objects on the tray. The activity is repeated and one of the objects is removed without the player watching. The player has to guess the object that has been removed.

Practise this game with objects from your pencil case. Make a tally of your success rate against a classmate, recording how many attempts each of you had and which object had been removed. Use your results to identify which type of memory will eventually be improved by this activity.

2 a Copy and complete the sequence that will lead to long-term memory, selecting from the phrases below:

Changes in the nerve cells

Short-term memory created

Repetition

Nerve pathway permanent

Nerve pathway created

b Old people sometimes develop a condition called **dementia**, where in the early stages of the disease they find it difficult to complete everyday tasks. What type of memory is affected by dementia?

c Explain why teachers do not encourage students to carry out copying exercises.

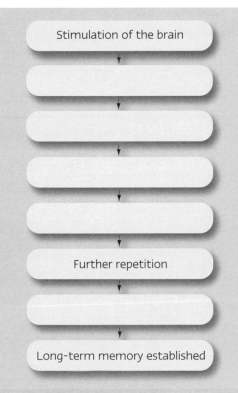

3 Electronic 'brain training' games claim that they can improve your memory. Design a digital game to improve the memory of students revising for their Science examinations. Your game must be fun, stimulating and offer the opportunity for the repetition of activities. Produce a set of instructions for your game, explaining how it will improve the user's memory.

See pages 32–33 of your Pupil Book

Effective learning

1 Drivers must commit road signs to their long-term memory so that they can drive safely. They may not see a particular sign for many months but they must instantly recognise and understand the sign so that they can react and drive with care and consideration for other motorists.

It is your task to use technology (such as your computer, mobile phone or MP3 player) to learn the road signs from the Highway Code and try to commit them to your long-term memory. Develop your own system of learning so that you can pass a mock theory test on the road signs next lesson!

2 Teachers use a variety of teaching methods to help you learn.

a Copy and complete the diagram by filling in the numbered boxes with the learning terms selected from the key words below.

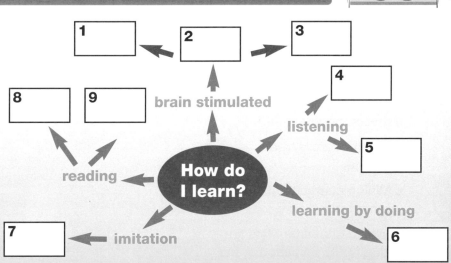

Passive   Short term   Long term   Visual   Auditory   Kinaesthetic   Memory

b List **four** different types of activity that a Science teacher may use to add variety to a lesson to stimulate the different types of learner in the class.

c Produce a visual mind map for revising the topic of nerves and nerve pathways.

3 Select a recent topic in science to revise. Create a quiz about your chosen topic to post on your school network. Your quiz must include scientific facts, figures and applications of the topic in everyday life. Pair up with a classmate and revise eachother's topic using the technique that suits your learning style – visual, auditory or kinaesthetic – and produce a visual mind map. Use the quiz to decide if your style of revision was successful and how you could improve the learning method for the next topic.

Why are we different?

1 Use a photograph of yourself to indicate what factors (such as eye colour, height, and attached or detached ear lobes) you have inherited from your parents and what factors are due to environmental influences (such as muscles you may have developed or even scars due to bumps and scrapes!). Make up a family tree of photographs of inherited factors and environmental influences.

Alternatively, you can investigate the features caused by inheritance and by the environment in a famous family (such as the Royal family) and create a family tree using photographs cut from newspapers and magazines.

2 We inherit characteristics from both our parents; however, the environment is also responsible for causing differences between people.

▲ Female with blue eyes

■ Male with brown eyes

Study the family tree opposite.

Sarah is tall and a very good netball player

John

Sarah   Jack

John is tall, athletic and a good swimmer

a Which characteristics are inherited?

b Which characteristics are due to the influence of the environment?

c Sarah is a member of a netball team. Is her skill at netball due to factors that are inherited, environmental or a mixture of inherited and environmental factors?

d Jack and Sarah are twins. Will Jack be a good basketball player? Explain your answer.

e Although Jack and Sarah are brother and sister, they have inherited different genetic information from their parents. Explain why genetic variation is important.

3 The 'Habsburg chin' was a prevalent physical characteristic in the Austrian dynasty. Use the Internet to research the causes of the genetic characteristics, explaining the disadvantages of the inherited trait.

Produce a PowerPoint ready for your next lesson illustrating your findings.

See pages 42–43 of your Pupil Book

How tall is this group?

Digital

1 The results in the table opposite were obtained when studying variation in a Year 9 class.

Length of little finger on left hand (mm)	Number of students
40–44	2
45–49	7
50–54	10
55–59	6
60–64	4
65–69	2

a Use Excel to plot a bar chart of the results.

b Explain how the investigator would have carried out their investigation, including why they chose the ranges of measurements shown in the chart and how they ensured that they were accurate when taking measurements. Do you think that this study is a good measure of variation in Year 9 students?

c Present your write-up as a PowerPoint.

Test yourself

2 A Year 9 class measures the height of all of the students in the class and places them into ranges, as shown in the results chart below.

Height (cm)	110-119	120-139	140-159	160-179	180-199
Number of students	2	10	8	7	0

a Plot a graph of the results.

b Which height range has the largest number of students?

c Why might the class results not match the national trend in average height of Year 9 students?

d Suggest how the method of recording the results could be improved.

e Suggest other methods for measuring variation between students in Year 9.

Creative

3 Design a prompt sheet to explain the meaning of the terms **reliability**, **accuracy** and **precision**.

Use a number of different sources to research these terms and include illustrations on your prompt sheet (to help you explain how to use scientific equipment). Your prompt sheet can then act as 'Top Tips' for these important terms when planning and carrying out your experiments.

What can twins tell us?

1 **a** How do you know that the twins in the photograph are not identical?

   b i In studies of identical twins, some sets of twins can have different physical features. Which of the following features are most likely to be different?

   eye colour

   gender

   nose shape

   hair colour

   attached or unattached ear lobes

   ii Explain your answer.

   c If twins are separated at birth, why is it that they are likely to be dissimilar?

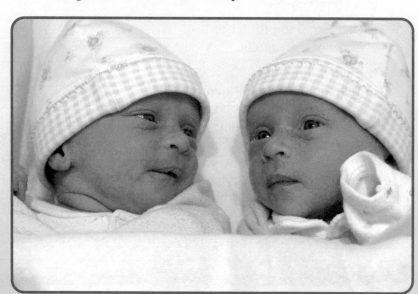

2 Create a poster for a classroom display on genetics, showing the eggs and sperm at each stage of fertilisation and how they produce:

   a identical twins (clearly displaying why they are genetically identical)

   b triplets, where **two** of the triplets are genetically identical.

3 Imagine that when you grow up you discover from browsing on Facebook that you have a long-lost twin!

Create a podcast to introduce yourself to your twin and examine how your case contributes to scientific debates about twins. In your podcast you must describe the genetic similarities between you, explain how environmental influences in your lives have made you different and discuss how your case could be used as an example in the nature versus nurture debate.

Hint: You may wish to use the Internet to research studies of twins to help you to compile your own case study.

It came from my parents

1   **a** Join the words to the definitions.

Nucleus	Fusion of male and female sex cells
Genes	Carry genetic information
Sperm	Structure located in a cell that contains chromosomes
Fertilisation	Male sex cell
Sex cells	Carries two sets of genes
Cheek cell	Carry one set of genes from each parent

b Which organs produce the male and female sex cells?

c In humans how many chromosomes are found in:

    i   a sperm cell   **ii**   an egg cell   **iii**   a fertilised egg cell   **iv**   a nerve cell?

d Why does a baby have characteristics from both parents?

2 Your teacher sets you the task of producing a PowerPoint to explain how the following organisms reproduce by sexual reproduction or by cell division:

    strawberry plant   **aphids**   **amoeba**   **frogs**

Use the Internet to find the information that you need for your PowerPoint. Post your work on your school network so that other students can use it to revise this subject.

3 You are studying the prediction of traits in humans. Your task is to create a set of examination questions on how certain traits are inherited. Consider:

- how the following dominant traits are inherited: unattached ear lobes, dark hair, curly hair, dimples
- how recessive genes are inherited
- what incomplete dominance means and whether it can be predicted

Swap your examination with a classmate. You must include genetic cross diagrams in your examination questions and prepare the answers to your examination so that you can mark your classmate's work. In addition, you must prepare imaginative explanations to your answers, so that your classmate can learn about genetics in a new way.

VARIATION PROJECT

Farmers have an interest in developing the animals and plants on their farm in order to produce quality food.

Imagine that you are a geneticist who has been called in to advise a farmer on breeding techniques and maximising crop yield. It is your role to advise the farmer upon each of his following suggestions, basing your opinion not only upon scientific facts but also upon the ethics of his suggestions.

1 The farmer loves his rare breed Gloucestershire Old Spot pig but is thinking of bringing in a new breed where the offspring will be all the same and will all produce the same quality of meat.

FIGURE 1: A Gloucestershire Old Spot pig feeding her piglets.

FIGURE 2: Oilseed rape seeds contain an oil that is used in vegetable oil, animal feed and biodiesel.

2 The farmer has heard of a new oilseed rape plant that is resistant to the effects of weedkillers. The farmer is worried that the gene from the oilseed rape may pass into the wild, creating a new 'super weed' similar to the Japanese knotweed which has spread rapidly and is difficult to get rid of.

3 The farmer is thinking of cloning his favourite old sheep that has produced many high quality lambs.

FIGURE 3: Why would the farmer want to clone his favourite sheep?

FIGURE 4: How would the farmer use surrogacy to breed his best dairy cow?

4 The farmer wishes to breed from his best milk cow by using her as a surrogate mother.

5 The farmer jokingly mentions that he is going to inbreed his sheep dog so that the puppies will be good sheep dogs.

Use your Pupil Book, library and the Internet to research your answers and produce your recommendations as a manual of advice for the farmer.

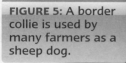

FIGURE 5: A border collie is used by many farmers as a sheep dog.

See pages 42–55 of your Pupil Book

Natural clones

1 Imagine that you are a researcher for the Radio 4 programme 'Gardeners' Question Time'. A listener telephones the panel to ask how she can take advantage of the natural cloning of runners in her garden. The presenters explain that information on today's questions can be found on the programme's website.

Create and complete the mock webpage on the right to answer the gardener's question.

Natural cloning

strawberry plants

spider plants

2 Owners who cannot bear the loss of the companionship of their much-loved cats when they die can now have them cloned. In 2004 a company in the U.S.A. cloned pet cats for $50 000! Write a letter to the Royal Society of Genetics expressing your feelings about this practice. It is important that your letter contains scientific facts about cloning.

3 **a** Copy and complete the sequence for cloning a sheep, using the phrases below:

   Egg cell transplanted into female sheep to grow

   Nucleus from sheep B placed into egg cell of sheep A

   Nucleus of cell removed

   Nucleus removed

   b When cloning plants, a cutting from the parent plant can be taken and planted in soil to grow. Why does the cutting look the same as the parent plant?

   c Cloning is used in fruit and vegetable production. What are the advantages of this cloning to the farmer and supermarkets?

   d What is the main disadvantage of cloning?

   e What are the economic advantages of cloning?

   f Explain why there are ethical concerns about cloning.

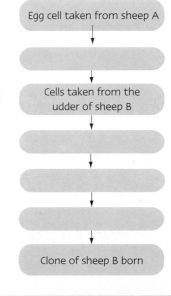

Egg cell taken from sheep A

↓

Cells taken from the udder of sheep B

↓

↓

↓

Clone of sheep B born

Dog breeding

1 Dogs have played an important part in man's history. Selective breeding has enabled man to breed a vast array of dogs for working and sporting purposes as well as breeding dogs for pets.

Use the Internet to research the different breeds of dog in order to design a new webpage for the Kennel Club. Your site must show: a photograph of the dog, its role, in what ways the dog is genetically adapted to its particular role, and how its distinctive features have evolved.

FIGURE 6: A dog working as a guide dog for the blind.

2 **a** Dogs and horses are two animals with a common ancestor. What is this common ancestor?

b i What is the type of selection called where characteristics are bred into an animal?

   ii What is the disadvantage of this method of breeding?

c Man has bred dogs for different roles throughout history. Name **three** of the different roles carried out by dogs.

d What is the advantage of breeding different types of dogs?

e Explain how breeding is used to select and breed a desired feature into pedigree dogs.

FIGURE 7: Man has not bred specific characteristics into this dog – she is the natural crossbreed of two terrier dogs.

3 In 2009 the BBC did not broadcast the world-famous Kennel Club Crufts dog show after an investigation concluded that dogs on the show suffer from genetic diseases following years of inbreeding.

Write a newspaper article that either supports the BBC's decision to halt the broadcasting or to give your support to the Kennel Club. Be sure to discuss the ethics of inbreeding to win Kennel Club awards and to give specific genetic examples in a named breed of dog.

See pages 54–55 of your Pupil Book

The alkali metals

Creative

1 Imagine that you are the senior laboratory technician in your school responsible for the storage of the alkali metals. Produce a set of clear instructions detailing how each of the metals in Group I should be stored and explaining the reasons for the precautions taken.

Test yourself

2 a Copy and complete the following sentences, choosing from the key words below.

less	sodium	three	similar	most
more	Group I	silvery	dissimilar	
alkali	Group II	dull	least	

Lithium, …………... , potassium and rubidium are the first four elements in …………... , the …………….. metals. The first …………….. of these metals are …………… dense than water and float on the surface. They are …………... when cut but tarnish when in air. Lithium is the …………... reactive and rubidium is the …………... reactive of the four. All four metals have …………... properties.

b i Identify the metals from the descriptions of their reaction with water, below:

Metal A: Floats on the surface of the water and a gas fizzes around it.

Metal B: Melts immediately on contact with water and the gas catches alight with a lilac flame.

Metal C: Melts as it whizzes across the surface of the water and the gas fizzes quickly.

ii Place the metals in order of reactivity, starting with the least reactive.

c Use your copy of the Periodic Table to identify **two** other metals that should behave in a similar way.

Digital

3 Imagine that you are the presenter of a children's science TV programme. On the show you will demonstrate reactions of alkali metals with water while informing the young audience of the scientific facts behind the demonstration.

Use PowerPoint to produce a film storyboard for your programme. Include the following in your storyboard: scientific information about alkali metals; why some alkali metals are unusual; information on using the reactivity trend to make predictions about the violence of each reaction; and health and safety.

Hint: http://video.google.com and www.youtube.com will provide some exciting ideas for your storyboard.

Word and symbol equations

1 Use Internet image sites to produce a dynamic display for your laboratory on describing chemical reactions. Present your display to the class with an imaginative poem, song or rap, using the key words on the right. Don't forget to rehearse your work – you may be asked to perform next lesson!

reaction   product   solid   heat

gas   dissolved   reactants   fizz

colour   equation   new material   pop

2 a Copy and complete the following sentences choosing from the key words below:

one   reactants   different   two   products   similar   reaction   new

A chemical .... takes place between .... or more .... , combining to form one or more .... and .... substances (the .... of the reaction).

b Identify the products and reactants in the following reaction:

sodium + water ⟶ sodium hydroxide + hydrogen

c i Alkali metals burn when heated in oxygen to form a white oxide. Complete the following word equation:

sodium + oxygen ⟶ ....

ii Identify the reactants and new compound in this reaction.

3 Produce a 'starter' for the next lesson on the 'Golden Rules' for recognising products and reactants, recognising patterns in chemical equations and understanding how to produce symbol equations.

Consider: how best to display your work to help the class learn about word and symbol equations, which illustrations you should use to demonstrate your 'Golden Rules', and which equations you will construct as examples.

Hint: You may wish to use some of the following examples:

- iron + oxygen ⟶ iron oxide

- magnesium + oxygen ⟶ magnesium oxide

- magnesium + hydrochloric acid ⟶ magnesium chloride + hydrogen

- zinc + hydrochloric acid ⟶ zinc chloride + hydrogen

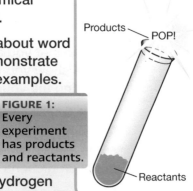

FIGURE 1: Every experiment has products and reactants.

Products — POP!

Reactants

Reacting metals

Digital (HSW) 4-5

1 Calcium and magnesium are so boring!

It is your task to produce **two** 'Amazing Fact' wikis on these metals. Include important information about these metals alongside interesting facts that will stun your friends and link the two metals! Make your work exciting and dynamic with illustrations and post it as a wiki with a maximum of 200 words.

Hint: The following website may be useful: www.facts-about.org.uk

Creative (HSW) 5-6

2 Your teacher is about to demonstrate the two experiments shown in question **3**. It is your task to produce the Hazcard for the experiment. You must detail the word equations for the two reactions, mention the precautions that should be taken and also include the appropriate hazard symbols.

Test yourself 7-8

3 Two experiments are set out as shown below.

a What gas is formed in both experiments **A** and **B**?

b How would you test the gas in Experiment **A**?

c If the contents of the beaker in Experiment **A** were filtered, and drops of litmus solution added, what would be observed?

d Name the solution formed in Experiment **A**.

e If a lighted splint is placed near the exit of the delivery tube in Experiment **B**, what would be observed?

f Write out the symbol equations for the two reactions.

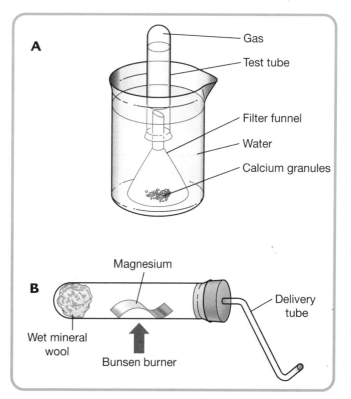

Metals and acids

1 Your teacher provides you with the following equipment to investigate the reaction between dilute hydrochloric acid and different metals: 3 test tubes; beaker containing 60 cm³ hydrochloric acid; aluminium, zinc, copper; measuring cylinder; stop clock. Plan your investigation, explaining: what you will do, what you will measure, what you will look for, how you will make it a fair test and how you will make it safe. Then, draw out your results charts with the correct headings and units.

2 You are set the task of comparing the rate of reaction of magnesium and calcium when placed in dilute hydrochloric acid. When the magnesium is added to the acid, bubbles of gas are collected and you record the results shown in the table below.

a Plot the points as a line graph.

b How much gas is produced between 10 seconds and 30 seconds?

c What happens after 40 seconds?

d Unfortunately you run out of time and cannot complete the reaction with calcium.

   i Predict your result by sketching the graph as it would look if the experiment was repeated with calcium.

   ii Using your graph, determine which metal – magnesium or calcium – would be first in the reactivity series.

e Construct the word equation for the reaction of magnesium with dilute hydrochloric acid.

Time (s)	Volume (cm³)
0	0
5	60
10	105
15	130
20	155
25	175
30	185
40	200
50	200

3 Research the reactions of potassium, zinc, sodium and magnesium with different acids (www.sciencepark.etacude.com is a useful site to begin your research). Then create a PowerPoint that the whole class could use to revise the chemical reactions that occur when metals are added to dilute acids.

Hint: Your revision PowerPoint should include fill-in-the-gaps equations, opportunities to develop powers of prediction and questions to test general knowledge of the topic.

Magnesium

Potassium

Sodium

Zinc

CHEMICAL PATTERNS PROJECT

Precious metals, diamonds and crystal gemstones have always played an important part in fashion and in displaying wealth and status. Throughout the ages, a variety of metals have been used in the manufacture of jewellery from gold, silver and platinum, through to nickel and copper.

Imagine that you manufacture jewellery for a studio specialising in vintage or historical design. You have been asked to create a guide to your manufacturing process in order to educate new employees about the science behind your designs!

FIGURE 2:

Copper

1   Design a piece (or set) of jewellery. As part of your design process you should consider the role that jewellery has played throughout history.

Hint: By visiting the Victoria and Albert Museum website you will be able to begin your research into your design: www.vam.ac.uk (go to the South Kensington site and view the Fashion, Jewellery & Accessories collections). Here it is possible to study jewellery through the ages as well as to view videos showing how jewellery is made.

Gold

Platinum

2   Create a leaflet that showcases your jewellery design. Your leaflet should highlight and explain:

- the stages in your design method

- the metal(s) you have chosen and why

- how your jewellery can be cleaned and polished safely

- how to display your jewellery (including the conditions under which it should be kept).

Silver

Remember to include in your leaflet any equations that will help you in your explanation.

3   Next, create a step-by-step guide to be posted in the workshop that shows how you manufacture your design and explains the role that science plays in each stage of the process, from design through to the final piece of jewellery.

Remember to include relevant equations in your guide.

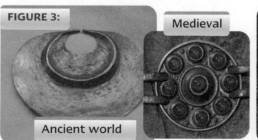

FIGURE 3:

Medieval

Ancient world

Victorian

1920s

Modern

See pages 62–81 of your Pupil Book

Acid concentration

4-5

Digital

1. The Dental Council has advised parents of the damage caused to teeth by sugary, acidic fruit drinks. These drinks are too concentrated and cause tooth decay.

   Imagine that you are a chemist working in the fruit drinks industry. It is your task to design a fruit concentrate drinks bottle that will allow parents to measure out the drink in a sensible concentration. Create a TV advert from your work that will explain how the bottle design prevents parents and children from preparing drinks that are too concentrated. Record your advert as a podcast.

   Hint: Use the following information on concentration to help you – 2 g of citric acid in 100 cm^3 water is double the concentration when 1 g of citric acid is used.

Creative

HSW

5-6

2. Prepare a role play that uses the particle theory to demonstrate how the rate of reaction of magnesium with hydrochloric acid is affected by the concentration and temperature of the acid. You will need to write out your script in full and gather together a few props as part of your preparation.

Test yourself

7-8

3. A piece of magnesium was placed into test tubes containing 20 cm^3 of hydrochloric acid of different concentrations. The volume of gas was recorded.

   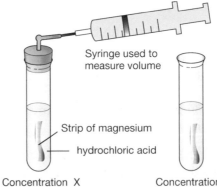

   Syringe used to measure volume

   Strip of magnesium

   hydrochloric acid

   Concentration X   Concentration Y

   FIGURE 4: Apparatus for testing the reaction of magnesium with dilute hydrochloric acid.

   a i What is the word equation for the reaction?

      ii What is the symbol equation for the reaction?

   A graph of the results was plotted (Figure 4).

   b Which acid was the most concentrated, **X** or **Y**?

   c Is the rate of reaction greater at **A** or **B**?

   d What conclusion can you make about the change in reaction speed (rate) with the concentration of acid?

   e Explain why the graph eventually levels off.

   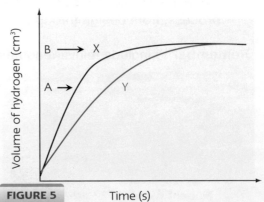

   FIGURE 5

   Volume of hydrogen (cm^3)

   B → X

   A → Y

   Time (s)

Displacement of metals

Creative

1 Write an imaginative and amusing illustrated drama about the Potassium family who are constantly struggling for supremacy! A selection of key words has been provided below:

reactive	metals	more	less	copper sulphate
magnesium	displaced	kicked out	coats	higher
lower	salt	reaction	bully	

You could begin your story with the main character:

'Mr Potassium was a bully…'

Test yourself

2 A metal is added to two different salt solutions. The reactions are shown below:

Salt solution	Metal X
Copper sulphate	Becomes coated in copper
Zinc sulphate	Becomes coated in zinc

a Identify metal X.

b If copper was added to zinc sulphate, would there be a reaction? Explain your answer.

c Write out the word equation for the displacement of iron in copper sulphate.

d What observations would you see in this reaction to tell you that a displacement reaction had taken place?

e Place copper, iron, zinc and metal X in order of reactivity.

Digital

3 Metal strips are added to different salt solutions:

- Copper into zinc sulphate ($ZnSO_{4(aq)}$)
- Zinc into iron sulphate ($FeSO_{4(aq)}$)
- Iron into copper sulphate ($CuSO_{4(aq)}$)
- Magnesium into zinc sulphate ($ZnSO_{4(aq)}$)
- Magnesium into copper sulphate ($CuSO_{4(aq)}$)

Construct the word and symbol equations for each reaction, then divide each equation into reactants and products. Using the two halves of your equations, create a digital matching card game. Play a classmate and compete to match the reactants in the displacement reaction with the correct products.

Predicting reactions

1 'Paper, Rock, Scissors' is a competitive game where players try to guess their partner's next move. Design your own game where the opponent has to predict the metal in the reactivity series to displace the metal that you reveal. Create a set of cards based on metals in the reactivity series for use in your game. Devise a scoring system that awards an extra mark for the answer where the metal is only one place higher in the reactivity series.

2 In the reactivity series the following elements appear in the order shown below:

$$\text{copper} \longrightarrow \text{mercury} \longrightarrow \text{gold}$$

a Copper and silver jewellery eventually tarnish if left in air, whereas gold does not. Predict where silver should be placed in the reactivity series.

b When iron ore (iron oxide) is heated with carbon, the iron is extracted from the ore. Explain why.

c Aluminium will displace iron from iron oxide. Predict which of the metals below could also be displaced by aluminium.

> **sodium**   **zinc**   **magnesium**   **tin**

d Large blocks of zinc are bolted onto the hulls of steel ships to protect the ship from the corrosive effects of sea water – the zinc is said to be sacrificed to protect the iron in the hull of the ship. Why is this possible?

3 Use the Internet to research the thermite reaction and how it is used in industry to join railway tracks together. Present your work as a wiki, including:

- the metals used
- a description of the reaction (with an explanation of the displacement process)
- the word and symbol equation for the reaction
- precautions taken during the spectacular reaction
- the industrial application of the reaction.

Hint: www.youtube.com is a useful site for viewing videos of the amazing reaction.

FIGURE 6: The thermite reaction.

Corrosion of metals

1   **a** Connect each of the metals below to the correct usage.

Gold	**Used to make jewellery**
Titanium	**Used for making cooking foil**
Stainless steel	**Used to manufacture electrical connections in computers**
Aluminium	**Used in stainless steel to manufacture cutlery**
Platinum	**Used in replacement body parts**
Chromium and nickel	**Used for surfaces in hospital operating theatres**

  b What evidence is there that gold and platinum are at the bottom of the reactivity series?

  c Why is tin used to coat metal cans?

  d Name **two** metals that do not corrode away and can be used for the roofing of buildings.

  e If aluminium does not rust, why are the majority of cars made from steel?

2   Rust is a huge problem in the airline industry: aeroplanes that are not in use will rust away if they are not protected.

Use the Internet to research where airlines park up their aeroplanes to protect the steel parts and explain how this tactic works. Display your work as a wiki, explaining why the airline industry uses this location.

FIGURE 7: Aeroplanes on stand-by.

3   In winter local councils salt the roads to lower the melting point of ice and reduce accidents caused by skidding on ice. When drivers return from their journeys they may park their cars in warm garages. This might not be the best advice if rust is to be prevented from attacking the metal body of the vehicle.

Design an experiment in which you maximise rusting to prove that the warm garage is not the best environment to prevent the car from rusting. You must:

- Draw out the equipment, showing it in use.
- Write your plan, including the control variable.
- Predict your results.
- Explain why steel and iron are used in the manufacture of cars, even though they rust. Is there an alternative material that could be used?

How to stop corrosion

1 **a** Why is rusting a problem in the car industry?

 b The experiment on the right is set up to determine the conditions needed for rusting.

| A | B | C | D |

Iron nail in water | Iron nail in boiled water | Painted iron nail in water | Iron nail in test tube with calcium chloride – absorbs moisture from the air

  i In which test tube will the iron nail rust?

  ii Explain why the iron nails will not rust in the other test tubes.

  iii List the conditions needed for rusting.

  iv This experiment lacks a control. How would the control for this experiment be set up?

  v If one of the nails was replaced with a galvanised nail, why would it not go rusty?

2 As an entrepreneur you decide to launch a company producing a range of attractive vases and drinking cups from anodised aluminium. Produce a website for your company displaying your new product and explaining the processes used in manufacture. Use the Internet to research the method used.

FIGURE 8: Colourful anodised beakers.

3 Imagine that you are a manufacturer of metal garden furniture, which will be exposed to the elements throughout the seasons. You decide to launch a new, modern range of brightly-coloured designs.

Present your designs as a leaflet to distribute at garden centres. In your leaflet you must explain how your furniture is protected to prevent it from rusting. Use a variety of innovative techniques, including painting, plastic coating, galvanising and anodising in your new eye-catching designs.

Metals and non-metals

1 **a** Which of the following are properties of metals?

   A Shiny when polished

   B Have low densities

   C Break easily when hit with a hammer

   D Poor conductors of electricity

   E Malleable

   b What is special about the metals iron, nickel and cobalt?

   c Tungsten has a melting point of 3400 °C. Why is this metal similar to most other metals?

   d What is unusual about the element carbon?

   e Why is graphite a suitable material to use in pencils?

Creative
HSW 5-6

2 Gather together a selection of **five** kitchen appliances and utensils (such as saucepans, spoons and an electric kettle). Make a simple drawing of each appliance and then produce a brainstorm for each appliance to identify the metals and non-metals used, the properties of these materials and why they are used in the manufacture. Use a selection of key words such as:

conductor　　**insulator**　　**electricity**　　**shiny**　　**strong**

FIGURE 3: An electric kettle.

FIGURE 1: Saucepans must be made of a material that conducts heat.

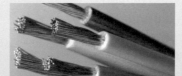

FIGURE 2: Metal wires inside electrical appliances conduct electricity.

Digital
HSW 7-8

3 You may think that graphite is only used in pencils and diamonds are only found in rings, but they aren't!

Use the Internet to research the structure of graphite and diamond, and relate this to their properties and applications. Then use your research to produce an illustrated wiki.

Acids, alkalis and bases

Digital 4–5

1 Dyspepsia (more commonly known as indigestion) is caused by excess stomach acid. Imagine that you are a TV advertising company working on a new advert for indigestion tablets. Use PowerPoint to produce a script and storyboard for your advertisement. Be sure to focus your advertisement on how the tablets work.

Test yourself 5–6

2 **a** When we have indigestion we take Seltzer tablets or Milk of Magnesia which contain a base to neutralise the acid in the stomach. What are these soluble bases called?

b i When an acid is neutralised by a base, a salt and water are produced. Complete the word equation for the reaction below:

sulphuric acid + sodium hydroxide ⟶ .... + ...

ii What is the pH after the reaction?

c Arrange the products and reactants below to produce a salt:

sulphuric acid ⟶ **potassium sulphate**

potassium hydroxide **water**

Creative HSW 7–8

3 Bee sting venom is formic acid (methanoic acid) and can be neutralised with calamine lotion (which contains zinc carbonate) or baking soda (which contains sodium hydrogen carbonate). In a similar way, a farmer carries out the neutralisation of soil that is too acidic by adding quicklime (calcium oxide), slaked lime (calcium hydroxide) or chalk (calcium carbonate).

FIGURE 4: Bee stings can trigger severe allergic reactions in some people.

FIGURE 5: A farmer adding lime to soil.

Produce an information leaflet for the lotion used to neutralise a bee sting and for the neutralising chemical used on acidic soil. Your leaflet must include a description of how the product works and an explanation of the neutralisation process (with balanced neutralisation equations). Use the rules below to help you to construct your equations:

acid + metal oxide ⟶ metal salt + water

acid + metal hydroxide ⟶ metal salt + water

acid + metal carbonate ⟶ metal salt + water + carbon dioxide

Carbonates and acids

4-5

Test yourself

1 Zinc carbonate is a base that can be used to neutralise an acid.

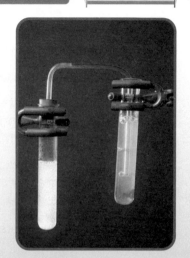

a The gas from the reaction is bubbled into an indicator liquid in the test tube, as shown on the right. Identify:

  i the gas

  ii the indicator liquid

  iii the evidence that the gas is present.

b If the solution is filtered to remove the excess zinc carbonate and tested using blue litmus paper, what would you expect to observe?

c What would this indicate has happened in the reaction?

Digital

HSW

5-6

2 When hydrochloric acid is added to limestone, the mass of the reactant decreases once the reaction is completed. Create a resource file for your school network that a teacher can use to demonstrate and explain this experiment. You should include the following in your resource file:

- images of the equipment needed in the experiment

- a video of the experiment, downloaded from the Internet

- a worksheet for students that shows how the mass has changed and providing the reasons for this change

- the equation for the reaction

- **five** questions (with answers) to test other students' knowledge on the reactions of carbonates with acids.

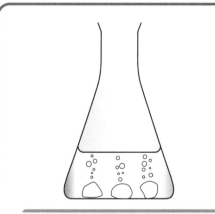

FIGURE 6: How do you know a reaction is taking place here?

Creative

HSW

7-8

3 Make models to show why the rate of reaction between solid zinc carbonate particles and dilute acid is quicker at increased concentrations and at higher temperatures. You could use dried peas, rice, dried pasta or dried beans to represent the particles of your reaction, displayed in a clear plastic food bag. Write up an explanation of your models using illustrations and key words to explain the differences in reaction times.

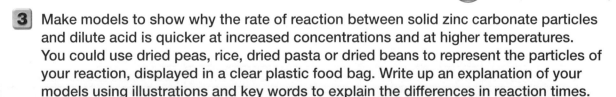

Salts

1 Produce an illustrated dominoes game to match examples of reactions between:

- an acid and a metal oxide
- an acid and an alkali
- an acid and a metal carbonate
- an acid and a metal.

Put the two reactants on one domino and the products on separate dominoes. Illustrate your dominoes and then devise a scoring system for your game. Play your dominoes game with a classmate to test your knowledge!

2 a Copy and complete the following sentences and equations using the key words below:

alkalis	metal	acid	acid
water	hydrogen	sodium	sodium chloride

   i Neutralisation of an .... by a base produces a salt:
.... + base ⟶ a salt + water. In this reaction the .... in the acid is replaced with a .... , as in the example with .... chloride.

   ii Hydrochloric acid + sodium hydroxide ⟶ .... + ...

b Name a use for the salt produced in the neutralisation reaction in part **a ii**.

c What type of salt is produced in a reaction between sulphuric acid and sodium hydroxide?

d When a salt is produced by neutralising an acid with an alkali, how would salt crystals be obtained from the solution?

3 a Use the Internet to research the formulae and uses of the different salts given in the table below.

b Continue your Internet research to find more examples of your own, including examples of water of crystallisation.

Complete your table in Excel and post it on the school network so that it can be used as a quick-reference guide by the whole class.

Salt	Formula	Type and number of atoms	Uses
	NaCl	1 atom of Na; 1 atom of Cl	Seasoning; preserving food
Calcium chloride		1 atom of calcium; 2 atoms of chlorine	
	NH_4Cl		Used in making batteries
	$CuSO_4.5H_2O$		

Making a salt

1 Use the Internet to research the methods used in the production of sodium chloride. Then, design an easy-to-follow PowerPoint that your teacher can use to explain how to produce this salt in the school laboratory by using neutralisation.

On your PowerPoint you must clearly show the word equation; a flow diagram showing the equipment to be used; stage-by-stage instructions for the production of the salt; and health and safety precautions.

Creative 5-6

2 Imagine that you are the quiz master on a children's game show. You must prepare a set of questions on making salts for the science section of the show. The show's producer has partly prepared two questions. You must now complete the answers and write a further **ten** questions (with answers).

i acid + base ⟶ .... + ...

ii Name the missing salt, base or acid:

Base / acid	Salt produced by reaction with...		
	Hydrochloric acid	**Sulphuric acid**	**Nitric acid**
	Calcium chloride		
Zinc sulphate		Zinc sulphate	
Sodium hydroxide	Sodium chloride		
Iron oxide			Iron nitrate

Test yourself 7-8

3 **a** Copy and complete the following statements:

Hydrochloric acid produces .... salts. Sulphuric acid produces .... salts. Nitric acid produces .... salts.

b i Write the symbol and word equations to summarise the neutralisation reaction between hydrochloric acid and sodium hydroxide.

ii What is the name of this type of reaction?

iii What process is used to remove the water in this reaction?

c The salts above are made by reacting an acid with an alkali. Write out the word and balanced symbol equations for an example of the reactions between:

i an acid and insoluble base ii an acid and metal.

d Give a named example of salt formed from:

i nitric acid ii sulphuric acid iii hydrochloric acid.

Imagine that you are an entrepreneur and decide to set up a small business making crystals to sell to schools and gift shops.

In order to establish your business and fulfil the necessary health and safety requirements you have drawn up the following plan of action:

Splint

Support thread

Seed crystal

Copper sulphate

1   Select and order the chemicals needed to produce the crystals.

2   Order in the equipment needed in the manufacture of your crystals (including any health and safety equipment).

3   Produce a set of clear instructions for your assistant worker, detailing how the crystals will be produced.

Remember you must include all relevant word and symbol equations in your instructions!

4   Produce a risk assessment for the Health and Safety Committee.

5   Purchase the correct hazard warning signs along with the Hazcards.

Hazard	Risk	Action

danger to the environment

toxic

highly flammable

irritant

risk of electric shock

You must now carry out your plan of action so that you are ready to launch your business!

FIGURE 7: Hazard warning signs used in industry.

Remember to use a combination of the Internet and science books to research the production techniques that you will use.

Precipitating salts

1 When hydrochloric acid is added to sodium thiosulphate a reaction occurs and the mixture slowly turns cloudy, producing a solid called a 'precipitate'.

The rate of the reaction is recorded and then repeated at different temperatures.

a Where on the graph is the rate of reaction the greatest?

b What trend can you see in the reaction?

c How would you make sure that the investigation is a fair test?

d Predict the rate at which the precipitate will be produced when the concentration of hydrochloric acid is increased.

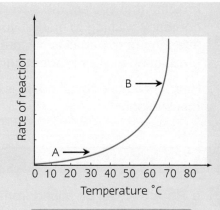

FIGURE 8: Graph of results.

2 Produce a set of matching reaction cards to test a classmate's knowledge of how precipitation can be used to form salts. Be sure to illustrate your cards using imaginative pictures that will help the reactions to stick in your classmate's memory!

You may like to consider the following reactions, or think of examples of your own:

- Copper sulphate + barium chloride → ....
- Sodium chloride + silver nitrate → ....
- Barium chloride + potassium sulphate → ....
- Cobalt chloride + sodium carbonate → ....
- Potassium sulphate + barium chloride → ....
- Copper nitrate + sodium carbonate → ....

3 Using research carried out online, produce a timeline showing the development of the production of paint pigments (highlighting the period when precipitation was used to produce artists' paints). Present your work as it would appear on the History department's webpage, in a new section called 'The development of science in industry and art'.

Hint: www.madehow.com will assist in your research.

Using salts

1 Imagine that you are the advertising manager for a sea salt company wishing to market your product to chefs. Design an attachment to e-mail to restaurants, providing details on the production of your product and the different salts in your product.

Hint: www.maldonsalt.co.uk is a good place to research this subject.

2 **a** Rock salt can be mined from the ground and is a mixture of salt and sand. Describe the method that is used to extract the salt.

b Some rock salts are pink in colour and cannot be purified into white salt by filtration and evaporation. Suggest a reason for this.

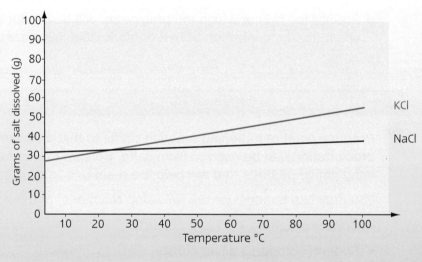

c The graph opposite shows the solubility of two different salts – potassium chloride (KCl) and sodium chloride (NaCl). By studying the graph determine which salt solution, if left to evaporate, will form crystals first?

d Calcium carbonate is an insoluble salt. How could it be separated from water?

3 In the next lesson your teacher is planning to purify rock salt. They request that you produce the practical instruction sheet for this activity.

Your instruction sheet should be based around a flow chart. On your flow chart you must detail when and how each piece of the equipment will be used, describe and explain the procedures at each stage and give the health and safety precautions that must be taken at each stage.

Your instruction sheet must also incorporate the balanced symbol equation for the reaction, with an explanation of what this equation means.

Pressure points

1 Design a poster for a classroom display on pressure. Use cartoons to show how area and pressure are related and to demonstrate useful applications of pressure.

Here are some examples that you could include on your poster: skis, a camel walking in soft sand, a sharp knife slicing food and firefighters rescuing a person who has fallen through the ice in a frozen pond.

2 It is your task to determine what will cause the most damage – a woman walking across a wooden floor wearing stiletto high heels or an elephant.

Hints:

- You will need to first research the average: mass of an adult elephant, area of an elephant's foot, mass of an adult woman and area of a stiletto heel.

- You must also consider how many feet the elephant has on the floor when walking compared to a human.

- Page 111 of your Pupil Book shows you a calculation that will help you to work out your answer.

- Use your knowledge of how pressure is applied to inform your answer.

Present your work as a PowerPoint that you can use to argue your case next lesson.

3 **a** Which block exerts the least pressure?

b If a nail has an area at the point of 2 mm² and the pressure exerted by the point is 20 N/mm², calculate the force used to strike the nail with a hammer.

c Why are women sometimes requested to remove their stiletto shoes before walking on a wooden floor? Explain your answer.

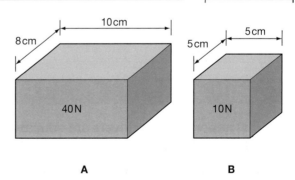

A   B

d If the point of a drawing pin has an area of 0.2 mm² and a force of 20 N is exerted by the point, what will be the pressure at the point? Give your answer in N/m².

e A stone block has a weight of 600 N and exerts a pressure of 240 N/m² on the ground. If the base of the block is rectangular with a length of 2 m, calculate the width of the block.

Pressure in gases

1 Imagine that you are a mountain guide in the Himalayas. Before the climbers arrive for their climb up the steep slopes you decide to make a model to explain why the atmospheric pressure decreases as they climb higher and why it is necessary for them to wear oxygen masks as they near the peak of the highest mountain.

You must create a model for your explanation – you could use dried rice, peas or beans to represent the air particles and a paper cone to represent the mountain. You must also prepare a script for your introductory talk.

2
a What is responsible for causing the air pressure inside the balloon?

b i If the sides of the balloon are squashed together, what will happen to the air particles inside the balloon?

ii What will happen to the pressure inside the balloon? Explain your answer.

c Apart from squashing the sides of the balloon, what is another method of increasing the pressure inside the balloon?

3 It is important that drivers are educated about the importance of correct tyre pressures.

a Use the Internet to research the correct tyre pressure for a selection of vehicles, perhaps your family's or your neighbour's car, or a motorbike. (Hint: many tyre companies will allow you to enter the registration of the vehicle to give the correct pressure – www.kwik-fit.com is one such site.)

b Using the research (and examples) that you have found, design a section that could be added to all car manuals to effectively inform the public of the importance of driving at the correct tyre pressure. Remember, your new section must demonstrate the science behind your advice!

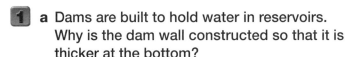

Pressure in liquids

1 a Dams are built to hold water in reservoirs. Why is the dam wall constructed so that it is thicker at the bottom?

b Why must divers not dive too deep when scuba diving?

c i Draw the jets as the water empties from the can (Figure 2).

ii From which hole does the water travel the furthest?

iii Explain your answer.

d If a balloon is filled with water and squashed, what would happen to the space between the water particles?

e i When the plastic bag full of water (Figure 3) is squeezed, water comes out in all directions. What does this tell us about pressure in liquids?

ii If the holes in the bag were all at the same depth, what could we learn about pressure in liquids from watching the water pour out?

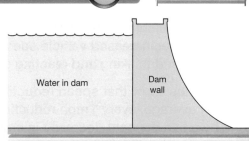

FIGURE 1: An illustration of a dam wall.

Water in dam · Dam wall

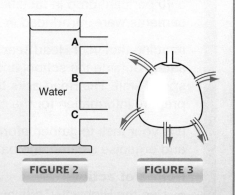

Water · A · B · C

FIGURE 2 · **FIGURE 3**

2 Imagine that you are a car mechanic and need to explain to your customers how the hydraulic braking system works.

Create a diagram similar to that shown opposite. Add to it the labels and scientific details that will help you to explain to your customers how their hydraulic braking system works. Choose an inventive and effective way to display this information to your customers!

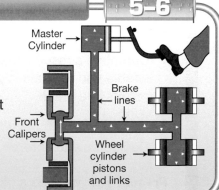

Master Cylinder · Brake lines · Front Calipers · Wheel cylinder pistons and links

3 Scuba diving is a dangerous sport if divers are unaware of the risks of diving too deep. Diving too deeply and quickly can lead to problems with breathing, tooth pain and a condition called the 'bends' (caused by absorbing nitrogen into the blood).

Use the Internet to research the dangers of scuba diving. Use your research to design a webpage aimed at using science to warn teenagers of the dangers of scuba diving and how to scuba dive safely.

PRESSURE, FORCES AND MOMENTS PROJECT

20 mph Speed Limit!

It is reported on www.slower-speeds.org.uk that speed is the biggest single contributory factor in road crashes. The reason is simple: increased vehicle speeds are not accompanied by increased thinking and reacting speeds.

Studies show that speed reductions cut casualties. On average, every 1 mph reduction in speed is accompanied by a five per cent decrease in crashes and a seven per cent decrease in fatalities. A ten per cent drop in speeds resulted in a 40 per cent drop in fatalities and serious injuries after speed cameras were introduced in West London.

Imagine that your Head Teacher is concerned about road safety outside the school and wishes to introduce a 20 mph speed limit. The Head asks the Science department to prepare information for the campaign.

It is your task to gather information from a variety of sources and organise a campaign based upon scientific facts.

Points of action:

- Use the Highway Code and Internet to gather information on thinking distances and braking distances at various speeds.

- Plan a survey to conduct on the speed of cars travelling along the road near your school, detailing the measurements that you will take.

- Carry out your survey.

- Complete a results chart. (Hint: 1 m/s = 2.24 mph – this will enable you to convert your results into mph.) Interpret your results in a graph.

- Plan the location of the speed limit sign.

- Decide how to enforce the new speed limit effectively.

Present your work as a high-impact document, including evidence of calculations and use of scientific terms, in readiness for the Head to use as part of the road safety campaign.

Turning forces and moments

1 Imagine that you are a novelty toy designer. You decide to add a balancing toy (such as the one shown opposite) to your toy range. Design your new toy along with a customer information label explaining how it works using turning forces.

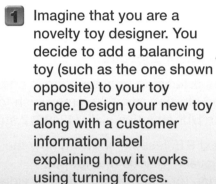
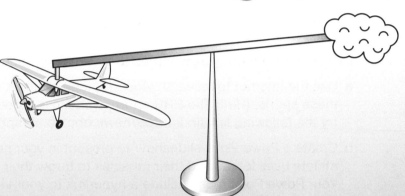

2 Medieval siege engines were used to launch huge boulders over the walls of castles. Design your own medieval war computer game where points are scored for launching 10 kg, 15 kg and 20 kg boulders the greatest distance! Use PowerPoint to produce a storyboard illustrating one or two scenes from your exciting game.

You must also provide a print-out of the packaging of your game. Be sure to use moments on the packaging to explain how to maximise the launch distance and gain extra points.

3 The model crane is used to lift the toy car (Figure 4).

a What must be done to the sliding weight to balance the crane?

b If the sliding weight is located 40 cm from the pivot when the beam is balanced horizontally, what is the turning moment?

c What is the unit for the turning moment?

d Using the principle of moments, calculate the weight of the car when the crane is horizontal and the toy car is 10 cm from the pivot.

e Explain in terms of the principle of moments why wine glasses have a wide base.

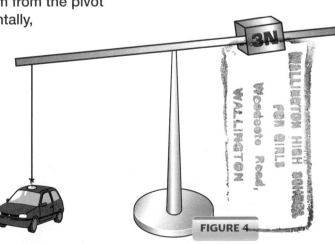

FIGURE 4

The Body Machine

1 In P.E., biology and physics come together to allow the body to perform a number of athletic activities.

Explain how the body uses forces to throw a javelin, discus or shot put.

a Use the Internet to research video footage of athletes practising or competing in one of these sports. (Hint: The BBC sports website is a good starting point. You may wish to try the following link first: http://news.bbc.co.uk/sport1/hi/athletics/skills/4249912.stm)

b Create a PowerPoint slideshow to present in your next P.E. lesson, showing how the athlete uses forces and their muscles to throw their javelin, discus or shot put. Your PowerPoint must include a hyperlink to your video (or a screenshot of your video) and a diagram with force arrows to show the direction of movement of the arms during the throw.

2
a Name the muscle that the weight lifter will use to lift the weight.

b Copy the diagram on the right and draw in a force arrow to show the force of gravity acting upon the weight.

c On your diagram draw in a force arrow to show the direction of the pulling force of the muscle.

d Name the muscle that will support the weight when the weight is lowered.

e When the arm moves, the muscles work in pairs to create movement. What is this called?

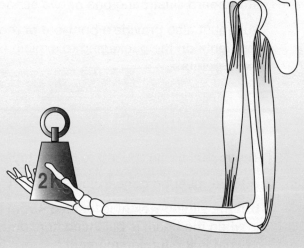

3 The Design and Technology department has asked the Science department to produce a display on levers and their applications in the home, garden and industry. You are assigned the task of producing a poster to show the applications of first, second and third order levers. Be sure to label your diagrams and draw in the force arrows correctly.

Hint: If you have access to the Internet you could research levers at www.automata.co.uk/leavers.htm.

Speedy sums

1

  a The car travels a distance of 200 m in 5 seconds. Calculate the speed of the car.

  b If the car is travelling at a steady speed will the forces be balanced or unbalanced?

  c The walker completes a hill walk in 3 hours at an average speed of 2 mph. Calculate the distance of the walk.

  d Why is the speed of the walker described as an 'average' speed?

2 Imagine that you are a County Council planner and decide to complete a survey comparing the average speed of school children as they travel to school by walking, cycling, public transport and car.

Ask your class about the details of their journey to school and complete the survey below.

Remember 30 minutes = 0.5 hour; 15 minutes = 0.25 hour; 5 minutes = 0.0833 hour

Mode of travel	Distance (miles)	Time (hours)	Average speed (mph)
Walking			
Public transport			
Cycling			
Car			

Write the conclusion to your survey as it would appear in the local newspaper.

3 Imagine that you are the producer of the television programme 'Top Gear' and wish to compare the performance of a range of cars, other high-speed modes of transport and members of the animal kingdom.

You must produce a storyboard of your show that includes comparisons of top speeds and acceleration rates, and force arrows to show if the forces involved are balanced or unbalanced. Then, film a short podcast to explain the key ideas in your show in an amusing and informative way!

The following websites will assist you in researching this exciting topic:

- www.geocities.com/dtmcbride/misc/speed-acceleration.html
- www.carspecsdirectory.com

Distance–time graphs

1 Using Excel, plot a distance–time graph for the following vehicle's journey:

Time (s)	10	20	30	40	50	60	70
Distance (m)	100	200	240	300	375	400	400

Use the graph to:

- Determine the period of time when the vehicle is travelling at its fastest.
- Describe the journey.

Post your answers on your school network, ready for your teacher to mark.

2 This graph shows the journey of a cyclist.

a Identify each part of the journey, matching the descriptions to the letters.

Stops for lunch

Cycling along a level road

Riding downhill

Riding uphill

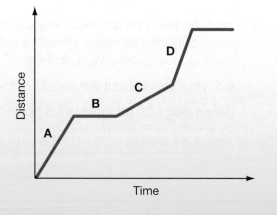

b Sketch the graph of the following bus journey from a town centre:

The bus slowly leaves the bus station in the town centre and stops at traffic lights. It travels quickly to the first bus stop, before halting at a road junction. It then joins a slow-moving traffic jam. It finally stops at the second bus stop.

3 Either: Imagine that you are the pilot of a search-and-rescue helicopter flying to assist a mountaineer who is stranded on a cliff face. Write the pilot's log for the rescue flight, detailing the stages (including speeds and altitudes) involved in the rescue mission. Draw the distance–time graph for the mission. Use your graph to calculate your speed when you were flying to the rescue site.

Or: Imagine that you are an F1 racing car driver completing a lap at the British Grand Prix. Talk through your lap over the radio to the pit crew, including details of the standing start, pit stop and passing the chequered flag! Draw the distance–time graph that would appear on the monitor in the pit lane. Use your graph to calculate your speed when you were travelling down the winning straight!

See pages 124–125 of your Pupil Book

Sources of light

1 **a** Copy and complete the sentences below using the key words listed.

translucent   **luminous**   **reflections**   **straight lines**   **emit**

opaque   **shiny**   **shadows**   **transparent**   **transfer**

The creation of .... relies upon the fact that light travels in .... and that light cannot travel through .... materials, but only through materials that are .... Our Sun is a .... star. Stars, fires and lamps all .... light.

b Copy the diagram below.

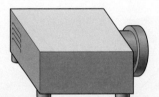

Projector

Screen

i Draw rays of light from the light source to show how the shadow is formed.

ii What are the **two** ways of making the shadow smaller?

iii Draw on the diagram to show how you would make the shadow larger.

2 Imagine that you are a clown hired for a children's party. Part of your act is to project animal shadows using your hands.

Draw **two** examples of animal shadows and produce a further diagram showing how you will project the shadows to vary their size. Present your work as part of an information leaflet for parents about your party acts.

3 Imagine that you are a radiographer taking X-rays of a child who has fallen off his bicycle.

Use the Internet to research the difference between X-rays and light rays, and to find images that support the findings from your research. Using your research, prepare a script with visual aids explaining to the child's parents what an X-ray is and how it identifies the injury.

Light and plane mirrors

1 Imagine that you design the paintwork for emergency service vehicles. You are asked to produce the lettering for the front of a police car, ambulance and fire engine so that the words can be read in the rear-view mirror of a car.

Sketch these vehicles and draw on the lettering as it would be seen by a driver looking in his rear-view mirror.

Test yourself — 5-6

2 a Complete the label boxes on a copy of the ray diagram (Figure 1).

b List **three** properties of the image.

c Complete the pathway of the ray of light in Figure 2.

d Copy and complete the diagram in Figure 3 to show the position of the image.

e What name is given to this type of image?

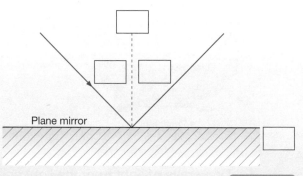

Plane mirror

FIGURE 1

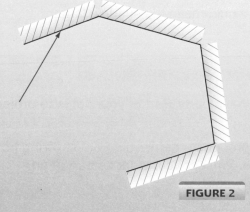

FIGURE 2

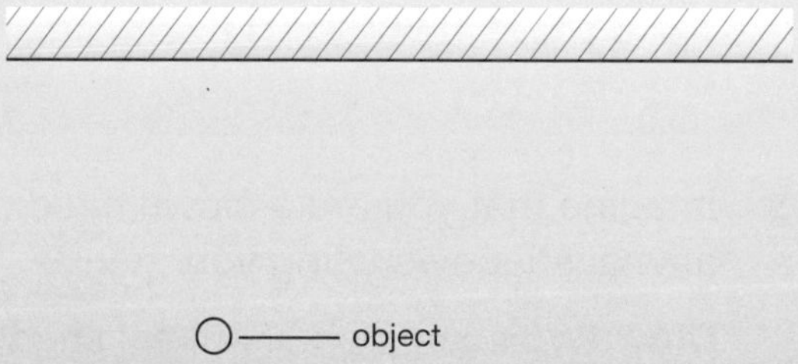

◯—— object

FIGURE 3

Digital — HSW — 7-8

3 You are going to watch a parade and realise that you may not be able to see because taller people may stand in front of you.

Design a periscope that will enable you to see. Present your design in the form of a Computer Aided Design (CAD) working drawing, clearly showing the angles of the mirror and how the rays of light will enter the eye. E-mail your design to the Resistant Materials Department for construction.

Curved mirrors

Creative HSW 4-5

1 Imagine that you are the security manager in the electrical department of a large department store.

Draw the shop floor layout to show the entrances, exits and escalators on your floor. Add to your floor layout the position that the curved security mirrors would have to be in to give you a view of the hidden recesses of the shop. Present your diagram as a working plan for the shop fitters who will position the mirrors.

Test yourself 5-6

2 **a** Identify the concave and convex mirrors in the diagrams opposite.

b Copy and complete the ray diagrams opposite by labelling the focal length and focal point.

c What are the properties of the image formed by a convex mirror?

d Why is a concave mirror used as a shaving mirror?

e Why are concave mirrors called 'converging mirrors'?

f Why are convex mirrors used as wing mirrors on cars?

A

B

Digital HSW 7-8

3 Imagine that you are a catalogue designer for a company that sells specialist mirrors. It is your task to produce a page in your sales catalogue using Microsoft Publisher (or similar). You must detail the different types of mirrors available, show photographs of the products from Internet image sites, explain their uses and give their specifications (including focal lengths in the case of curved mirrors).

Here are some examples of mirrors that you may wish to include:

- plane mirrors for use in shops and the home
- small plane mirrors for experiments in school Science lessons
- security mirrors for viewing the underside of vehicles
- shaving mirrors
- dental mirrors
- mirrors used in a solar furnace.

Total internal reflection

Creative   HSW   4–5

1 Small children and parents are often frightened by the technological equipment in hospitals.

Imagine that you are a doctor and you need to use an endoscope to view the inside of a young boy's lungs. Produce a child-friendly leaflet to reassure the patient and his parents by explaining how the optical fibres work in an endoscope.

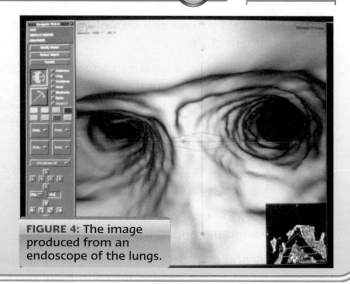

FIGURE 4: The image produced from an endoscope of the lungs.

Digital   5–6

2 The internal workings of optical devices are a mystery to most people.

Use the Internet to research images of optical devices (such as cameras, binoculars and periscopes). Download your images and add light rays to them to show the applications of total internal reflection. Produce an imaginative illuminated light display (where your light rays would be lit by coloured lights) for a camera shop to explain how total internal reflection is used in the prisms of cameras, binoculars and periscopes.

Test yourself   7–8

3 **a** Using the Law of reflection, complete the pathway of the ray of light as it passes down the fibre optic.

b What is an optical cable?

c Explain why there are two different sets of optical fibres in an endoscope.

d Endoscopes are used in hospitals to view the inside of the human body. Suggest a further use for the endoscope.

e What are the advantages of using optical cables instead of copper cables?

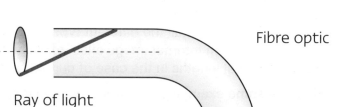

Fibre optic

Ray of light

Refraction

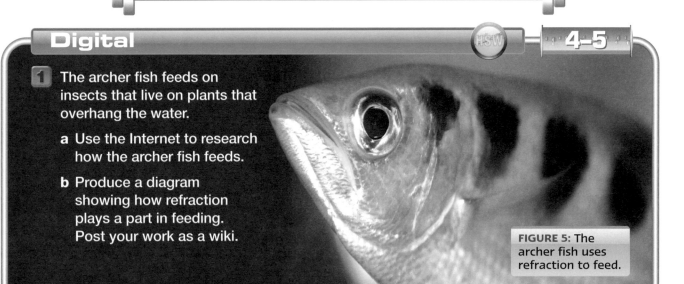

1. The archer fish feeds on insects that live on plants that overhang the water.

   a Use the Internet to research how the archer fish feeds.

   b Produce a diagram showing how refraction plays a part in feeding. Post your work as a wiki.

   FIGURE 5: The archer fish uses refraction to feed.

Test yourself

2. **a** Copy the diagrams in Figure 6 and complete the pathways of light through the glass blocks.

   b What is it called when light changes direction as it enters a glass block?

   c Select the correct options in the sentence below:

   When a ray of light enters denser transparent material it bends **away from/towards** the normal because the light is **speeded up/slowed down**.

   d Copy the diagram in Figure 7 and draw the position of the coin at the bottom of the beaker of water when viewed from above.

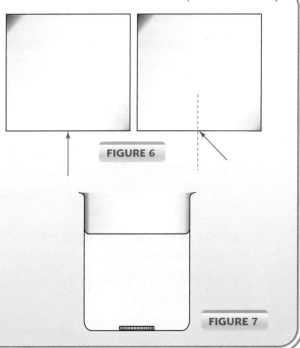

FIGURE 6

FIGURE 7

Creative

3. Produce an information leaflet for customers in an optician's office illustrating how convex and concave lenses are used in spectacles and contact lenses to correct vision defects. Your information leaflet must clearly explain how refraction is responsible for changing the direction of the light and focusing it on the retina at the back of the eye.

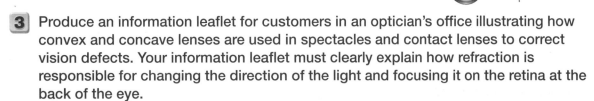

Isaac Newton 'the optickian'

1 Mirrors, lenses, prisms and optical cables are used in many optical devices.

Use the Internet to produce a timeline for use on the History department's webpage, linking the scientific development of these devices with historical inventors. Be sure to describe how these inventors came by their discoveries! Include examples such as microscopes, telescopes, spectacles, prisms and optical fibres.

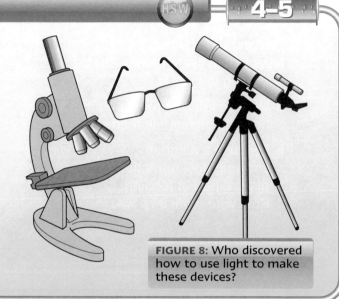

FIGURE 8: Who discovered how to use light to make these devices?

Test yourself 5-6

2 a i Copy and complete the diagram showing what happens to white light when it passes through a 60° prism.

ii Which colour of light will be located at position **1**?

iii Which colour of light will be located at position **7**?

iv Which colour of light is refracted by the prism the least?

b Why is the light refracted by different amounts?

c What name is given to the above phenomenon?

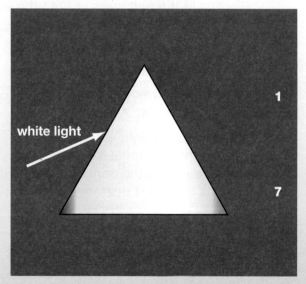

white light

1

7

Creative 7-8

3 Imagine that you are a lighting engineer working for a light show company. Use the phenomena of dispersion, reflection and refraction to design a light show projector.

Produce your design as a drawing and write a script to present it to the engineering department.

Colour

1 Produce an exciting and imaginative light show for use on an illuminated display in a city centre advertising milk, orange, lemon, lime and blackcurrant drinks. Show clearly how the light will be reflected from each product. Create your light show on the computer in Paint (or similar) and present it as the screensaver on the company computer.

Test yourself 5-6

2 **a** Explain why:

    i A white object is seen as white in white light.

    ii A red object is seen as red in white light.

  b Which colour of light will pass through each filter in Figure 9?

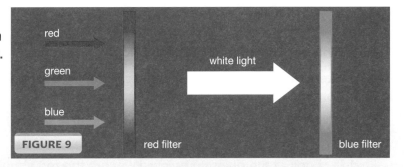

FIGURE 9

  c **i** Look at Figure 10. What colour will the red object appear after the light has passed through the green filter?

    ii Explain your answer to part **i**.

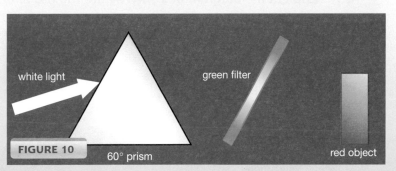

FIGURE 10   60° prism

Creative 7-8

3 Imagine that you are the lighting technician for an exciting and colourful pantomime.

Produce the lighting sequence for Act 1. In your sequence you must:

- show the coloured filters that you will use
- describe how you will combine filters
- give the order in which you will use the filters
- detail the colour of the costumes
- explain the reasons for your choices.

Present your work in the form of illustrated instructions for the lighting controller for the Act in the pantomime.

See pages 144–145 of your Pupil Book

Using colour

1 Imagine that you are a designer working for an advertising company. Your company's clients manufacture traffic lights, road signs, hazard warning signs, high visibility jackets, warning labels and red fire engines.

Produce a dramatic, eye-catching display for the company to show how they use colour in their products. Present your work as a podcast, giving a snapshot of your advertising campaign in preparation for the product launch.

2 a What are the primary colours in light?

b Sketch a diagram to show the secondary colours of light and how they are formed from the primary colours of light.

c Sketch a diagram to show how white light is formed from the primary colours of light.

d i Look at the diagram below. Why are the red shoes red in white light?

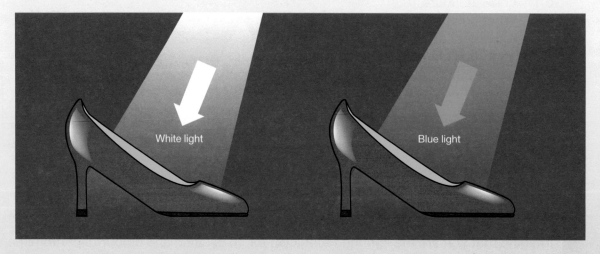

White light

Blue light

ii What colour will the red shoes appear in blue light? Explain your answer.

3 Imagine that you are a police officer attending a road traffic accident (RTA) in a city centre where the light from the colourful advertising hoardings flashes on and off and changes colour. You take statements from the passers-by and realise that there is conflicting evidence regarding the colour of the vehicles involved. Write a report explaining the reasons for these differences in evidence.

Seeing the light

4–5

Creative

1 The eagle, rabbit, owl, honeybee, chimpanzee and chameleon have eyes that are adapted to suit their habitat.

Produce a display for a zoo that examines the link between physics and biology. Illustrate your display and explain how a range of animals have different types of eyes, how the eye has evolved from earlier creatures and how the eye enables creatures to survive (especially when it comes to catching prey and reducing the chance of being eaten!).

Test yourself

5–6

2 **a** Copy the diagram in Figure 11. Draw a ray of light to show how the child is able to read the book using light from the lamp.

b Name the parts of the eye, **A–F**, in Figure 12.

c Which part of the eye:

  i Adjusts the amount of light entering the eye?

  ii Focuses the light onto the back of the eye?

d What is the name of the light-sensitive layer at the back of the eye?

e What is the role of the optic nerve?

FIGURE 11

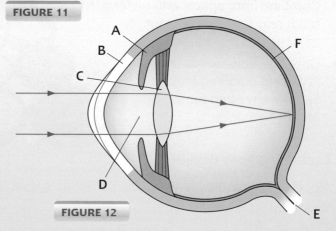

FIGURE 12

Digital

7–8

3 After conducting an eye test, an optician informs a patient that they are suffering from red-green colour blindness.

Use the Internet to research the causes of colour blindness and the different types. Produce a PowerPoint displaying the eye and highlighting the part affected in colour blindness, along with further details of your research.

ENERGY TRANSFERS PROJECT

Lighting design has changed considerably with the development of new technology.

Imagine that you are a lighting engineer designing new and innovative lights, including:

- hazard warning lights for car owners
- torches for mountaineers and sailors
- reflectors and lights for cyclists
- lamps fixed to a headband for plumbers, electricians and engineers to illuminate difficult-to-see places
- table lamps with multi-functions – perhaps as a reading lamp or providing background lighting.

Design development

It is your brief to design a new light that is exciting and dynamic! You must incorporate at least **two** technologies into your design.

Here are some ideas to get you started with your design:

- Combine a bright light with a diverging lens (with the option of coloured filters) to be used as a hazard warning lamp.
- Combine a set of prisms or cats eyes with a flashing coloured light for cyclists.
- Combine fibre optics with a standard torch and a concave mirror for an engineer.
- Combine fibre optics and revolving coloured filters in a novelty lamp for a child's bedroom.

Explaining your design

Along with your design you must complete a specifications booklet.

Your booklet must contain:

- details of where your lamp will be used
- explanations of how it works
- explanations of how it will be powered
- ray diagrams showing the pathway of the light
- details of the electrical circuit and, in some cases, how the brightness of the lamp is controlled.

Make your design interesting and dynamic, perhaps serving a special role in the home, industry or a hospital.

Resistance in circuits

Creative

1. Produce a script dramatising electrical resistance in the light bulb or electric kettle. Prepare a few props and write out your script, ready for your curtain call next lesson!

   Hint: You may wish to consider the idea of supporters entering a stadium through a turnstile or narrow roads at the end of a motorway.

Digital

2. Imagine that your company manufactures electrical appliances, including kettles, toasters and irons.

   Use the Internet to research the resistance of different thicknesses of Nichrome resistance wire used in the manufacture of heating elements. (Thicknesses of wire are given in Standard Wire Gauge, or SWG.) Present your findings as a catalogue in Microsoft Publisher (or similar). Include images of the appliances you manufacture, showing the position of the element in each appliance.

   Hint: www.greenweld.co.uk/acatalog/Shop_Nichrome_52.html is a useful site for your research. You could also use the Science department ordering catalogue for your research.

Test yourself

3. An investigation is carried out to find the relationship between resistance and length of wire. The following results are obtained:

Length of wire (cm)	Resistance (ohms)
8	16
6	12
4	8
2	4
0	0

   a i What is the independent variable in the investigation?

   ii What is the dependent variable in the investigation?

   b i Plot the results as a line graph.

   ii Use your graph to determine what happens to the value of the resistance of the wire if the length of the wire doubles.

   c Nichrome wire is used in the manufacture of elements in kettles, toasters and heaters. Suggest if this material has a lower or higher resistance than a length of copper wire of the same dimensions.

See pages 152–153 of your Pupil Book

Modelling circuits

1 Students are very often confused by the terms used in the teaching of electricity and their definitions:

voltage   current   resistance   electron   force   charge   carriers

Produce a game to help you and your classmates learn these terms. Present your work as it would appear in a 'drag and drop' interactive activity. Be sure to print off a copy of your answers!

2 Your Science teacher has been asked by the local primary school to hold an activity day based on electric circuits. As part of the visiting team you decide to make a model to explain how electric circuits work. In your model you must explain why increasing the number of cells in a circuit makes a lamp brighter and hotter.

3 An investigation is carried out to determine the relationship between electric current and voltage using a length of resistance wire.

   a i Use the results chart below to plot a graph of voltage against current.

Current (amps)	Voltage (volts)
0.1	2
0.2	4
0.3	6
0.4	8
0.5	10

   ii What is the relationship between voltage and current?

   iii Use the graph to find out what happens when the voltage is doubled.

  b What will be the value of the current if the voltage is increased to 16 V?

  c What would happen to the readings on the ammeter if the resistance wire used in the investigation was increased in thickness?

  d What precautions should be taken if completing this experiment with higher value resistance wire? Explain your answer.

  e What is the resistance of the wire when the voltage is 12 V and the current reading is 4 A?

See pages 154–155 of your Pupil Book

Using electricity

1 Imagine that you are a school student in the Victorian era when electricity was not widely available and you are transported forward in time in the Tardis time machine by Doctor Who!

Write a diary of the events of your day encountering new electrical devices, detailing the advantages gained through using each appliance and any problems that you see with relying on electrical devices. You might wish to consider some of the following aspects of your day: boiling water for a cup of tea, travelling to school, communicating with your friends with a mobile phone, working on a computer.

2 **a i** Copy and complete the table below to show the type of energy transferred in a number of appliances.

Appliance	Useful energy	Wasted energy
Light bulb		
Electric heater		
Electric hairdryer		
Electric drill		
Electric toaster		

   ii For each of the devices listed in part **i**, give an alternative method of completing the task that they fulfil.

b What are the advantages of using low-power electric light bulbs?

c Give **four** advantages gained from using electricity as a source of energy.

3 Imagine that you are a sales manager selling electric cars. Prepare a PowerPoint for a training session with your sales team so that they can explain how the electric car works, understand its advantages and disadvantages, and know the benefits of using this exciting new technology!

Use the Internet to search for information on this subject. www.howstuffworks.com/electric-car.htm is an excellent starting point.

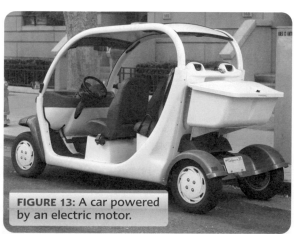

FIGURE 13: A car powered by an electric motor.

Electricity in the home

1 **a** Copy and complete the following sentences using the key words below:

second   hour   minute   heat   watts   light   Joules

The electric heater converts electrical energy into .... energy. The amount of energy the heater uses per .... is called its 'power'. Power is measured in ....

b Place the following appliances in order according to the amount of power they use:

A Low-energy light bulb **B** Electric cooker **C** Washing machine **D** Kettle **E** Light bulb

c Why is the government advising householders to replace their traditional light bulbs with low-energy bulbs?

d We can calculate the efficiency of an appliance by using the following formula:

$$\text{efficiency} = \frac{\text{useful energy output}}{\text{total energy input}} \times 100\%$$

Use the formula to calculate the efficiency of a washing machine if 1500 J of energy is used to wash the clothes and the total energy input is 2500 J.

2 Imagine that you are the manager of an electrical appliance store. The new stock of washing machines, dishwashers and tumble dryers has arrived but unfortunately the information detailing the efficiency of the appliances has not. You must first calculate the efficiency of each appliance:

Appliance	Useful energy (J)	Total energy input (J)	Efficiency (%)
Washing machine	1500	2500	
Dishwasher	1200	1800	
Tumble dryer	800	1700	

Now, produce an illustrated poster for your shop showing the efficiency of each appliance and explaining to the customers why purchasing energy-efficient appliances will assist with the sustainability of fossil fuels.

3 The government is eager that every household reduces its carbon footprint.

Imagine that you have been asked to produce a government advert to inform the public about how they can reduce their carbon footprint. Produce a podcast of your ideas along with a script for the Government Minister for Energy to view for approval. (Hint: www.direct.gov.uk/actonco2 will help you to research ideas.)

What resources do we need?

1
a Deforestation is the removal of forest. Why does man carry out this activity?

b Why is man increasing the areas of land where deforestation is carried out?

c Describe **two** ways in which deforestation damages the environment.

d i What **two** chemicals do farmers use on farm land? Explain the role of each.

  ii Describe how these two chemicals can lead to the pollution of our drinking water.

Digital 5–6

2 According to the RSPB, intensive farming has caused more damage to birds in Britain and Europe than any other single factor – including climate change.

Imagine that you are a reporter working for the RSPB with the task of justifying this statement. Produce a podcast in which you put your argument to a farmer who farms intensively to maximise the use of his land.

Creative 7–8

3 A newspaper reports that a second Channel Tunnel rail link is planned to run from Calais to London and on to Birmingham. This will be a fast train service cutting travel time to France and the rest of Europe.

Imagine that you are the Editor of the magazine '*Our Environment*'. Write a high-impact editorial article about the proposed rail link, focusing on the disadvantages of the new railway line.

Hint: The pictures below may help you to formulate an argument against building the new rail link (which may damage or even completely destroy habitats).

FIGURE 1: How would the construction of the rail line impact on environments such as woodland?

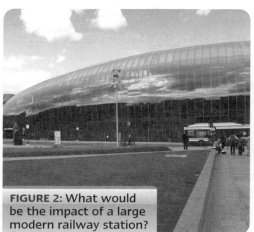
FIGURE 2: What would be the impact of a large modern railway station?

FIGURE 3: An indirect effect of the new rail line may be increased road networks and traffic.

The effect of acid on plants

Digital 4-5

1 Create a PowerPoint to explain the causes of acid rain. Include pictures as visual aids. (Hint: www.maltaweather.info/pollution.html will help you to research the key information on this subject.)

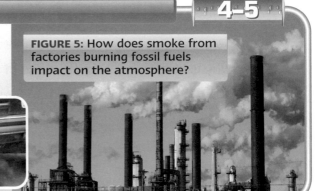

FIGURE 4: Car exhaust fumes contribute to the creation of acid rain.

FIGURE 5: How does smoke from factories burning fossil fuels impact on the atmosphere?

Test yourself HSW 5-6

2 The results charts opposite show the length of the shoot and root of plants grown in tap water and acid rain water.

   a i Use the results to find the average shoot and root length for plants grown in tap water and for plants grown in acid rain.

   ii Plot a bar chart of these averages.

   b What is the difference in average root and shoot length between the plants grown in tap water and those grown in acid rain water?

   c Name **two** gases that dissolved in the rain water and caused it to become acidic.

   d What effect will the acid rain have on the quality of crops grown in areas where there is acid rainfall?

   e How would you use your results to evaluate the evidence of the effects of growing plants in acid rain water?

Plants grown in tap water	
Length of shoot (mm)	Length of root (mm)
50	25
52	24
54	26
61	23
44	31
49	26
47	31
38	23
42	21
51	18

Plants grown in acid rain water	
Length of shoot (mm)	Length of root (mm)
34	20
42	19
48	17
48	14
43	12
36	15
32	16
40	21
41	13
34	18

Creative 7-8

3 Forests on high mountains in Scandinavian countries are damaged by acid rain. Create your own piece of dramatic artwork to illustrate the damage caused to a tree that has suffered the effects of acid rain, compared with a tree growing in a non-polluted atmosphere. Produce a fully-illustrated flow diagram to explain your artwork.

See pages 168–169 of your Pupil Book

How clean is our air?

1 Figure 6 shows two forms of the peppered moth found in Britain.

The light coloured moth is found in the countryside and is well camouflaged against the lichens and mosses growing on the tree trunks. During the Industrial Revolution a dark form of the moth appeared in the cities. This darker version was well-camouflaged against the darker bark on the trees. The moth is a food source for birds.

a What caused the bark on the trees to turn dark in colour during the Industrial Revolution in Britain?

b What was the origin of pollution during the Industrial Revolution and what form does this pollution take?

c Why was it an advantage for the moths in the city to be dark in colour?

d Today in Britain the darker type of moth is less common than the lighter-coloured moth. Suggest a reason for this.

FIGURE 6: A dark and light peppered moth.

2 It was reported by the United Nations in 2008 that there is a 3 km wide cloud of air pollution hanging over Asia. This sooty air pollution (called the 'brown cloud') has a major effect on human health, causing lung diseases such as bronchitis, cardiovascular problems and even increasing the risk of cancer.

Write a leaflet for a travel company advising holidaymakers of the dangers of this air pollution and the precautions they should take when visiting these countries.

3 Air pollution was a major concern for the Chinese government during the Beijing Olympic Games in 2008.

Imagine that you are a researcher for a children's news programme. Produce a simple storyboard for a two-minute report on the causes of the air pollution and the actions taken to control it at the Beijing Olympic Games. Record your report as a podcast.

Hint: Use the BBC website to collect your research.

HUMANS AND THE ENVIRONMENT PROJECT

Planet Earth is at a tipping point where the influence of man is affecting the biodiversity of the planet. It is estimated that 16 000 species of plants and animals are under threat of extinction due to the actions of humans. Halting the loss of this biodiversity by 2010 and beyond is a key concern of DEFRA – the Department for Environment and Rural Affairs (in the UK). The E.U. Heads of State have also agreed to halt the decline in biodiversity.

FIGURE 7: Animals in many different habitats are under threat, from tigers in forests and grassland areas to polar bears in the Arctic and gorillas in tropical forests.

FIGURE 8: How have humans affected biodiversity in key habitats, such as rainforests and coral reefs?

Imagine that you are part of a team organising a project to reverse the decline of biodiversity on a global scale. Before you can put your project into action and persuade governments around the world to support it, you must thoroughly research this important issue.

Your job is to:

1 Find out which key environments are under threat from man.

2 Explain why these environments are under threat.

3 List the animals and plants that are threatened in this habitat.

4 Explain how you plan to halt the decline in the habitat and maintain the biodiversity.

Research

The video on the following site shows the importance of maintaining biodiversity for the very wellbeing and continued existence of our species and is a useful site to begin your research:
www.youtube.com/watch?v=UotgGud9HKQ

http://archive.greenpeace.org/comms/cbio/bdfact.html and http://news.bbc.co.uk/1/hi/sci/tech/7361539.stm are also useful sites that will help you in your research by presenting you with different opinions on this issue.

FIGURE 9: Which human activities have put whales under threat?

Presentation

Present your work in the way that you think will be the most effective in persuading governments around the world to halt the decline in biodiversity before it is too late!

See pages 166–181 of your Pupil Book

What happened to the atmosphere?

4–5

Digital

1 Imagine that you are a scientist working in Antarctica to research the effect of the hole in the ozone layer.

Conduct research into this problem, using the website www.theozonehole.com (this is excellent for illustrations as well as providing video evidence). Write up your research, describing the ozone layer, how it is destroyed and the effects this has upon the human population.

Creative

5–6

HSW

2 Carbon dioxide, carbon monoxide, sulphur dioxide, CFCs and smoke particles are pollutants.

Produce a high-impact poster for a classroom display to show the origins of these forms of pollution (including the role that technology has played) and their effects on the planet. Include labelled illustrations along with scientific explanations to give your poster maximum impact.

FIGURE 10: Why does Shanghai have a problem with smog?

Test yourself

7–8

3 Since the Industrial Revolution the percentage of gases in the atmosphere has increased.

a Identify the gases that contribute to the greenhouse effect from the list below.

    oxygen   carbon dioxide   methane   nitrogen   nitrogen oxide

b What are the sources of each of the gases that you have identified?

c Use the diagram below to explain how the greenhouse effect leads to global warming.

d Explain the stages leading to global warming.

e It is important to take the temperatures related to global warming accurately. Why may taking temperatures in city centres lead to inaccuracies?

f CFC gases are released from refrigerators. What effect does the increase in CFC gases have upon the atmosphere and what are the potential hazards of this increase?

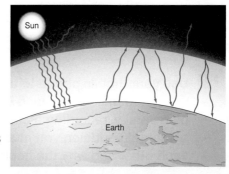

Looking at your surroundings

1 It is reported in your local newspaper that the council is selling the woodland near to your school for a housing and shopping development. Many children use the footpath along the boundary of the woodland on their way to and from school and it is the habitat of animals such as foxes and many species of plants.

The newspaper asks your school's Science department to carry out a survey of one species of plant in the wood as part of a campaign to halt the development. Write a report for the newspaper on the different techniques that you will use to measure the distribution of plants in the woodland and predict how this will help its cause!

2 During an investigation of plants on the verge around the edge of a school field, a 1 m^2 quadrat was used and the following readings recorded.

Quadrat	Dandelion	Daisy	Plantain	Clover	Buttercup
1	2	7	1	5	2
2	3	6	5	2	3
3	2	2	4	1	1
4	2	8	3	6	4
5	0	5	2	8	0
6	1	6	1	3	2
7	5	4	4	2	1
8	0	2	3	1	3
9	3	1	2	3	0
10	2	0	1	4	1

a Plot a bar chart to compare the total number of plants of each type.

b What was the total area of the verge sampled?

c What is the most common plant in the samples taken?

FIGURE 11:
From top: dandelion, daisy, plantain, clover, buttercup.

d Why is the sample only an estimation?

e If the total area of the verge around the edge of the school field is 1000 m^2, estimate how many buttercups would be found on the whole verge.

3 Use your mobile phone to take a video of an area of biodiversity – this may be woodland, fields, farmland or even your garden. Use the video to analyse the range of biodiversity, recording a commentary on the number of different plants and animals present. In addition you must explain how the animals and plants are dependent upon each other and why the habitat is important to humans.

Conservation

Test yourself 4–5

1
  a The osprey is a protected bird. The breeding sites of the osprey are kept secret and there are heavy fines for stealing their eggs. Some sites are even protected by CCTV. Explain the reasons for this level of protection.

  b The red squirrel cannot compete with the grey squirrel and as a result it is being forced out of its habitat and has become extinct in most areas of Britain. What action can be taken to re-establish small colonies of the red squirrel?

  c Why is deforestation a problem to some endangered species?

  d What action can be taken to preserve rare animals in areas where large-scale building is taking place?

Digital 5–6

2 Once a species of animal or plant is extinct, it is lost forever. Areas of the country are designated as special areas for protection under a number of different schemes:

SSSI, Ramsar, Biosphere Reserve, Nature Reserve and **AONB**.

Use the Internet to search for the definitions of these different types of site and explain the purpose of conservation in each case. Present your work as a wiki to be shared with your class.

Creative HSW 7–8

3 Cley Marshes on the Norfolk coast is a world-famous Nature Reserve. It is home to a wide variety of rare birds, plants and other animals. The fresh water lake where the birds live and feed is protected from the sea by a huge shingle ridge. Due to the very high cost of maintaining the ridge and surrounding areas the government will eventually allow the marshes to be flooded.

Produce a speech that you will deliver at a local council meeting expressing your point of view on this issue. Argue your case – either in favour of conservation or allowing the marshes to be flooded – using scientific fact to support your argument.

FIGURE 12: The fresh water lake at Cley Marshes.

Can we save the planet?

1 The following information compares the CO_2 emissions of travelling by air and car.

Mode of transport	CO_2 emissions (tonnes)
Small car per year	2.6
Single plane journey to Spain for two people	0.8
Single plane journey to the USA for two people	2.6

a Which mode of transport produces the greatest amount of carbon dioxide emissions (CO_2)?

b For how long could you drive your car before it produced the same CO_2 emissions as a plane journey to the USA?

c How many flights to Spain would be needed to produce the same CO_2 emissions as driving a small car for one year?

d How could car owners reduce their CO_2 emissions when driving a car?

2 The government has just announced its approval of a third runway at Heathrow Airport. Produce a campaign leaflet either in favour of or against the expansion of the airport, including scientific facts in your argument.

3 The UK fishing industry is in decline but the fishermen want to protect their jobs for future generations.

FIGURE 13: Can quotas save the UK fishing industry?

Research the proposals that are being put forward to protect the UK fishing industry. (Hint: these proposals include cutting the number and type of fish that the fishermen are allowed to catch.) Put yourself in the position of the fishermen and present your report as a video link from the trawler deck of a fishing boat.

Use the BBC website (www.bbc.co.uk) to begin your research.

See pages 180–181 of your Pupil Book

Studying sedimentary rocks

4-5

Test yourself

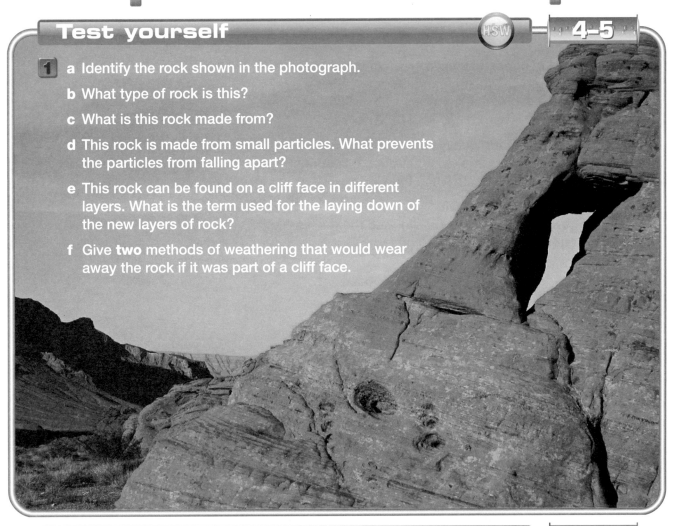

1 **a** Identify the rock shown in the photograph.

b What type of rock is this?

c What is this rock made from?

d This rock is made from small particles. What prevents the particles from falling apart?

e This rock can be found on a cliff face in different layers. What is the term used for the laying down of the new layers of rock?

f Give **two** methods of weathering that would wear away the rock if it was part of a cliff face.

Digital

5-6

2 Young children love building sand castles on the beach – but where does all of the sand come from? Many people believe that it comes from the sea, but it does not.

Research the origins of the sand on a beach and produce an animated slideshow to show the sequence of events from the source of the sand to the final sand castle on the beach!

Creative

7-8

3 Imagine that you are a supplier of stone for the building industry. Produce a leaflet illustrating the different types of rock that can be used in construction. It is important that the information supplied to your customers links the particle structure with the properties and uses of the stone.

More about sediments

1

a The map opposite shows areas of the country where coal fields are found. Suggest what may have been present in these areas millions of years ago.

b i Fossils of fern leaves are found in some coal samples. What does this suggest about the climate when the coal was formed?

ii Why did the plants that formed the fossils not rot away?

c i Suggest why coal is called a 'fossil fuel'.

ii Name another fossil fuel.

d How would you identify coal as a sedimentary rock?

Creative 5-6

2 Imagine that you are a palaeontologist who has been called upon to identify the fossil remains of a dinosaur.

Write about your find in your fieldwork notebook. You should include:

- a field sketch of the fossil

- notes about the rock type where the fossil was found

- details about the probable climate and types of vegetation that would have been in the area when the dinosaur was alive.

Digital 7-8

3 Rocks provide us with both a picture of what the Earth looked like millions of years ago and details of the climate at that time.

Use the Internet to research how different types of sedimentary rocks provide us with an opportunity to look back at prehistoric times. Produce a presentation (with visual aids) to show how the climate and environment of your favourite holiday destination has changed since prehistoric times. Be sure to use organic evidence such as fossils to explain the evidence for this change.

Hint: www.windows.ucar.edu/tour/link=/earth/geology/sed_facies.html will assist with your research.

GEOLOGY PROJECT

FIGURE 1: The fossil of a small dinosaur.

The Fossil Story

Fossils give us the opportunity to study prehistoric animals and plants, and also provide us with a window of opportunity to view the habitat and climate at that time.

Imagine that you are one of a team of palaeontologists studying the fossil in Figure 1. You must use the findings from your work to create a new display for the Natural History Museum.

Use the Internet to research fossil digs, where dinosaur fossils have been found and the types of rocks in which they have been found.

Recording and interpreting your findings

Create a field notebook to record your findings. You may wish to include:

- details of the location of the site

- details of the type of rock in which the fossil was found

- any conclusions you can draw from information about the rock (for example, igneous rock may provide evidence of a volcanic eruption)

- clues provided by fossilised plant remains

- evidence of the grisly death of the dinosaur

- how the dinosaur remains have been preserved.

Modelling your findings

FIGURE 2: What would the prehistoric environment of the dinosaurs have looked like?

Create a poster for the museum display to describe the life of the animal, its habitat and sources of food. Make your description exciting and full of scientific facts.

If you have time make a model of your animal fossil for show-and-tell at the museum. (You may wish to use Plaster of Paris, clay or Plasticine.)

Health and Safety: If using Plaster of Paris, do not use your hands to make the fossil shape when the plaster is setting. The chemical process releases heat and will cause severe burns.

Explaining your findings

Create a poster for the section of the display called 'The Wider Context'. You could consider the rock cycle, how different types of rocks are formed and how landscapes change.

Hint: Use the Internet and Science books to help you to explain the wider context.

Mountains and folds

1 Folds in rocks developed millions of years ago and can be seen in coastal cliffs.

Demonstrate the stages involved in this process with a novel demonstration using food! Design (or if possible make) a cake or sandwich that you can use to show how the folds in rocks occurred. Use different fillings and layers to shape the food and detail the forces you will need to finally demonstrate how folds are formed.

Test yourself

5-6

2 Look at the diagram opposite.

a Suggest what could have been responsible for causing the fault in the cliff face.

b Which strata in the rock face is the oldest?

c Fossils of sea creatures can be found in the rock of the cliff face. What does this suggest about what has happened to the land?

d Explain why the particles in the lower strata in the cliff face are very close together, forming a stable hard rock.

A

B

C

D

3 The Geography department has asked the Science department to prepare a presentation to convince its students that continental drift is responsible for the shaping of the continents that we are familiar with today.

Use the Internet to research how the shape of the continents has evolved. Armed with your research, create a jigsaw (either electronically or using card and coloured paper) showing how the continents once interlocked together. Produce notes for the teacher to use to explain how the continents have moved.

See pages 194–195 of your Pupil Book

Metamorphic rocks

Creative

1. It can be tricky to identify the different types of metamorphic rocks. Design a key (branching diagram) using questions to clearly link the features, properties and uses of **three** different types of metamorphic rock. Add to your key the details of the original rock and what has caused the rock to change.

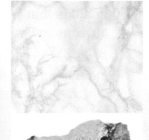

FIGURE 3: Slate, marble and quartzite

At the start of the next lesson, ask a classmate to use your key to identify the three rock types.

Digital

2. Imagine you are a designer with the brief to contribute to a brochure on kitchen and bathroom design where natural building materials are used.

Use the Internet to search for images of metamorphic rocks used in home design. Present your work in preparation for the brochure, detailing the properties of the materials used and why they are suitable in your designs.

Test yourself

3. a From what rock is the statue in Figure 4 sculpted?

   b In Figure 5, magma is shown rising through a layer of rock. The rock layer closest to the magma will become the metamorphic rock used for the statue. What is this layer of rock made from?

   c Suggest how the layer of rock closest to the magma is made.

   d Quartzite is a metamorphic rock formed from sandstone. How are the structural features of the rock related to its properties?

   e Apart from volcano sites where else may metamorphic rocks be formed and why?

FIGURE 4

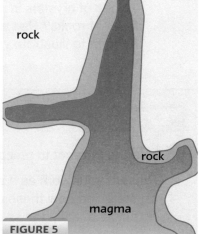

rock

rock

magma

FIGURE 5

Crystals in igneous rocks

Creative 4–5

1 Imagine that you own a gemstone shop selling crystals found in different igneous rocks.

Produce an illustrated plaque for a new display of **three** crystals. You must include information about the structure of the crystals and the conditions under which the crystals grew.

Test yourself 5–6

2 **a** Pillow basalt (shown in Figure 6) is made in underwater volcanoes. Suggest what size the crystals found in the pillow basalt will be.

b Suggest the conditions under which the quartz crystals were formed.

c In slate the crystals are flat. What does this suggest about the conditions under which they were formed?

d Metamorphic rocks are rich in crystals but do not have any fossils. Suggest the reason for this.

e What is similar about the shapes of crystals in different rocks? Use a diagram to illustrate your answer.

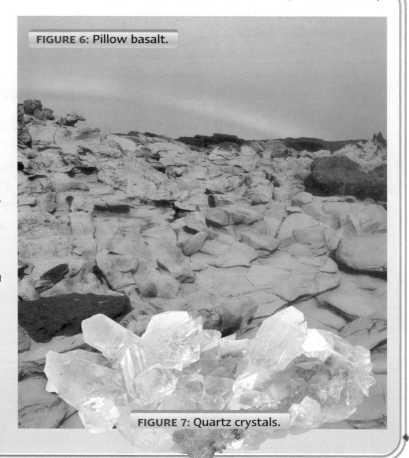

FIGURE 6: Pillow basalt.

FIGURE 7: Quartz crystals.

Digital 7–8

3 Use the Internet to research intrusive and extrusive crystal formation in igneous rocks.

Present your work as a wiki in order to explain the reason for the different sizes of crystals and how these crystals were formed in a range of metamorphic rocks (such as pillow basalt, gneiss and granite).

See pages 198–199 of your Pupil Book

Volcanic magic

1 Imagine that you are a volcanologist who has flown to report on a volcano that is about to erupt.

Produce a podcast of the report that you will give from the rim of the volcano as the eruption begins! You must describe the internal structure of the volcano and the processes of the eruption, as well as explaining the terminology to your audience as you make your escape!

Hint: www.windows.ucar.edu/windows.html will help you to research volcanic eruptions.

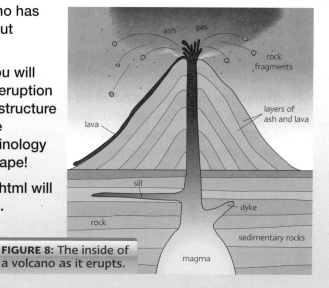

FIGURE 8: The inside of a volcano as it erupts.

2 The Geography department has invited the Science department to produce a display to show how different rocks and minerals are formed from volcanoes. Produce your display as a poster showing rock and mineral samples and detailing their formation.

3 **a** The formation of volcanoes takes place at subduction zones where one tectonic plate dips below another, as shown in the diagram opposite. Why does one plate dip below the other?

b What causes the rock to melt at these plate boundaries and form magma?

c How does magma go on to form a volcano?

d What causes the volcano to erupt?

e Why does the magma that is formed have a different composition to the two tectonic plates?

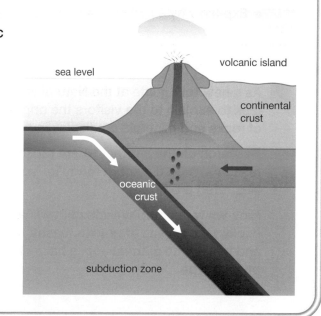

The rock cycle

1 Create a board game based upon the rock cycle:

Decide on the start point and the end point of your game (for example, a volcanic eruption).

The game may involve labelling the different aspects of the rock cycle or answering scientific questions to allow the players to move forward in the game.

Put a time limit of ten minutes on your game so that it may be used at the start of the next lesson to challenge your understanding of the rock cycle.

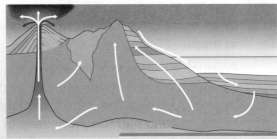

FIGURE 9: Here the arrows indicate how rocks form, are weathered, recycled and re-formed.

2

a Place the following in the correct sequence to explain how sedimentary rocks are formed:

b Igneous rocks are formed from magma. Where does the magma come from?

c What features will be found in the rock if the liquid rock magma cools quickly above ground?

d During transportation what will happen to the rocks?

e Explain why a sedimentary rock could be called a 'second-hand rock'.

sedimentary rocks	metamorphic rocks
deposition	erosion
weathering	transport
	sediments

3 As a new tour guide at the Natural History Museum it is your task to explain to the visitors the origins of the different types of rocks and minerals on display in the Geology section.

Research on the Internet where rocks come from. Using your research, record a script ready for your tour, along with illustrated prompts.

Hint: www.geography4kids.com will assist in your search to explain the origins of granite, basalt, marble, slate and gneiss and how some of these rocks have changed from their original type.

FIGURE 10: A violent volcanic eruption. The hot lava is clearly visible flowing down the side of the volcano.

See pages 202–203 of your Pupil Book

Notes

Notes

Acknowledgements

The Publishers gratefully acknowledge the following for permission to reproduce copyright material. Whilst every effort has been made to trace the copyright holders, in cases where this has been unsuccessful or if any have inadvertently been overlooked, the Publishers will be pleased to make the necessary arrangements at the first opportunity.

The Publishers would like to thank the following for permission to reproduce photographs:

p. 7 © iStockphoto.com / Gannet77; p. 8 © iStockphoto.com / Omer Sukru Goksu, © Zephyr / Science Photo Library; p. 11 © iStockphoto.com / Photo-Max; p. 12 © mushisushi – Fotolia.com, © Fesus Robert / 123rf.com, © SWT – Fotolia.com; p. 14 © iStockphoto.com / stockcam, © iStockphoto.com / lucato; p. 17 © Victor Spacewalker. Image from BigStockPhoto.com, © 210 / iStockphoto.com; p. 21 © iStockphoto.com / Michael Blackburn; p. 24 © Alan Carey / Science Photo Library, © iStockphoto.com / pastie, © Najlah Feanny / Corbis Saba, © Dan B. Image from BigStockPhoto.com, © iStockphoto.com / GlobalP; p. 25 © iStockphoto.com / Mark Sauerwein, © iStockphoto.com / Ling Xia; p. 26 © Boris Djuranovic – Fotolia.com, © and courtesy of Alexandra Riley; p. 30 © iStockphoto.com / cerae, © Charles D. Winters / Science Photo Library, © Andraz_Cerar. Image from BigStockPhoto.com, © david martyn. Image from BigStockPhoto.com; p. 31 © iStockphoto.com / Scott P. Orr, © Baloncici – Fotolia.com, © E.R.Degginger / Science Photo Library, © iStockphoto.com / 270770, © iStockphoto.com / Velezgreene, © iStockphoto.com / cenglanddesigns, © iStockphoto.com / subjug, © iStockphoto.com / jtyler, © iStockphoto.com / manley620; p. 34 © Charles D. Winters / Science Photo Library; p. 35 © iStockphoto.com / maikid; p. 36 © iStockphoto.com / Nicola Stratford; p. 37 © joegough. Image from BigStockPhoto.com, © demarco – Fotolia.com, © JackF. Image from BigStockPhoto.com; p. 38 © Dr Jeremy Burgess / Science Photo Library, © Jonathan Eastland. Image from BigStockPhoto.com; p. 39 © Andrew Lambert Photography / Science Photo Library; p. 42 © Eye of Science / Science Photo Library, © iStockphoto.com / pkruger; p. 44 © leaf. Image from BigStockPhoto.com; p. 48 © Fatman73 – Fotolia.com; p. 56 © Pascal Goetgheluck / Science Photo Library; p. 57 © SimKS. Image from BigStockPhoto.com; p. 62 © mandj98. Image from BigStockPhoto.com, estike.   from BigStockPhoto.com, © Ellende. Image from BigStockPhoto.com, © Yuuri. Image from BigStockPhoto.com, © mikle. Image from BigStockPhoto.com, © yurok. Image from BigStockPhoto.com; p. 65 © nruboc. Image from BigStockPhoto.com; p. 67 © Aleksander Bolbot / 123rf.com, © Tomasz Parys. Image from BigStockPhoto.com; p. 67 © haider. Image from BigStockPhoto.com; p. 68 © iStockphoto.com / webphotographeer, © iStockphoto.com / EvansArtsPhotography; p. 69 © Bill Coster IN / Alamy; p. 70 © iStockphoto.com / schnuddel, © Keith Levit / 123rf.com, © Fiona Ayerst / 123rf.com, © lsk. Image from BigStockPhoto.com, © Eli Shafer. Image from BigStockPhoto.com, © Brandon Cole Marine Photography / Alamy; p. 71 © Jeremy Walker / Science Photo Library; p. 72 © Alexey Lisovoy. Image from BigStockPhoto.com, © Martin Heaney. Image from BigStockPhoto.com, © Nigel Cattlin / Alamy, © Kris Langston. Image from BigStockPhoto.com, © Agnes Martelet. Image from BigStockPhoto.com; p. 73 © and courtesy of the author; p. 74 © iStockphoto.com / remem; p. 75 © BVDC – Fotolia.com; p. 77 © mg7. Image from BigStockPhoto.com; p. 79 © chrisroselli. Image from BigStockPhoto.com, © bilderbox – Fotolia.com, © iStockphoto.com / lissart, © iStockphoto.com / April30; p. 80 © Ingrid Stamatson / Alamy, © 2008 Jupiterimages Corporation; p. 82 © Beboy – Fotolia.com

Student Progress Card

Name: ....

Organisms, Behaviour and Health	4-5	5-6	7-8
Drugs and Behaviour			
What is a drug?			
Is alcohol really that good?			
A nail in the coffin			
Another nail in the coffin			
Cannabis			
Just say no			
Detecting your environment			
Being in control			
What are we born with?			
Learning behaviour in animals			
Aggression			
How do I learn?			
Effective learning			
Variation			
Why are we different?			
How tall is this group?			
What can twins tell us?			
It came from my parents			
Natural clones			
Dog breeding			

Chemical and Material Behaviour	4-5	5-6	7-8
Chemical Patterns			
The alkali metals			
Word and symbol equations			
Reacting metals			
Metals and acids			
Acid concentration			
Displacement of metals			
Predicting reactions			
Corrosion of metals			
How to stop corrosion			
Chemical Reactions			
Metals and non-metals			
Acids, alkalis and bases			
Carbonates and acids			
Salts			
Making a salt			
Precipitating salts			
Using salts			

Name: ....

Energy, Electricity and Forces	4-5	5-6	7-8
Pressure, Forces and Moments			
Pressure points			
Pressure in gases			
Pressure in liquids			
Turning forces and moments			
The Body Machine			
Speedy sums			
Distance-time graphs			
Energy Transfers			
Sources of light			
Light and plane mirrors			
Curved mirrors			
Total internal reflection			
Refraction			
Isaac Newton 'the optickian'			
Colour			
Using colour			
Seeing the light			
Resistance in circuits			
Modelling circuits			
Using electricity			
Electricity in the home			

The Environment, Earth and Universe	4-5	5-6	7-8
Humans and the Environment			
What resources do we need?			
The effect of acid on plants			
How clean is our air?			
What happened to the atmosphere?			
Looking at your surroundings			
Conservation			
Can we save the planet?			
Geology			
Studying sedimentary rocks			
More about sediments			
Mountains and folds			
Metamorphic rocks			
Crystals in igneous rocks			
Volcanic magic			
The rock cycle			

Topic 1 – Drugs and behaviour

What is a drug?

2 a Drugs are **chemicals** that alter the way in which your body behaves. Cocaine and **caffeine** are **stimulants** that increase brain activity whilst **depressants** such as **heroin** and **tranquillisers** slow down the nervous system. If addicts try to stop taking a drug they will suffer from withdrawal **symptoms** such as anxiety.

b Drugs slow down the body's ability to react quickly and therefore the driver may cause an accident.

c Caffeine stimulates the brain and will make sleeping difficult.

d Drug addicts are often so desperate for drugs that, if they have no money of their own to pay for drugs, they will resort to crime to fund their addiction.

Is alcohol really that good?

1 a The number of speeding drivers increases as the time of day increases, until 3 a.m.

b 75 – 60 = 15% increase

c People drink more in the evening than during the day. Some people will then try to drive home after a night out. After drinking, people will have less control of their vehicles or will drive recklessly as they think they are 'invincible'.

d Between 6 a.m. and 9 a.m. alcohol is still present in the blood of drivers who have been drinking the night before. Between 9 p.m. and midnight some drinkers will attempt to drive home after an evening out. The alcohol in their systems makes drivers more reckless on the road.

e At all times of day alcohol affects the judgement of drivers who have been drinking and as a result they speed when driving.

A nail in the coffin

3 a i The larger air sacs will reduce the surface area where the exchange of gases can take place.

ii This will lead to increased breathlessness.

b i oxygen + glucose ➡ carbon dioxide + water + energy

ii Emphysema prevents enough oxygen from getting into the blood, leading to lack of energy produced in respiration. This lack of energy will result in the leg muscles being unable to sustain movement up the flight of stairs.

c As emphysema prevents oxygen from being efficiently transported in the blood, the heart will need to work harder to circulate oxygen. This causes blood pressure to rise and heart disease will follow.

d Emphysema sufferers can use oxygen cylinders to breathe from when extra oxygen is needed.

Another nail in the coffin

1 a Cancer (39.7%)

b 41.3%

c 0.7% of passive smokers die of smoking-related diseases. Non-smokers should not be exposed to this risk in public buildings.

d i 'At risk' refers to the potential hazard (or chance) of being exposed to unfortunate consequences – in this case to the consequences of cigarette smoke.

ii The chart shows that there is a chance that the children of smokers will suffer from smoking-related diseases caused by passive smoking.

Cannabis

2 a 12 – 6 = 6%

b The potency of cannabis has increased over the eight-year period.

c The authorities are concerned because cannabis smokers may not be aware of the increased potency of cannabis and therefore not know that the effects of the drug are increased.

d The increased potency intensifies the effects of the cannabis on the user, including aggression, panic attacks, paranoia and damage to the memory.

e Users of the drug should be warned to reduce consumption to counteract the effects of increased potency.

Just say no

3 a 21% (accept 20%)

b Between 1995 and 2004 the number of drugs offered dipped sharply and then, mid-way through the period, increased sharply. The number of teenagers taking drugs sharply decreased just after the number of drugs offered began to decline, but increased slightly at the end of the period.

c The graph shows that the number of students taking drugs has only decreased slightly from its peak in 1995. Therefore the education programme between 1987 and 2004 has not reduced the percentage of students taking drugs, but in recent years it may have been a factor in stopping this percentage from increasing alongside the number of drugs offered.

d i Regular users of ecstasy will suffer from sleep problems, lack of energy and depression; it is associated with memory loss and emotional changes; in some cases one tablet has caused death.

Cocaine is associated with sweating, loss of appetite and increased pulse rate; snorting cocaine damages the membranes in the nose; regular use can cause restlessness, insomnia, weight loss and paranoia.

ii Students to give own reasoned answer.

Detecting your environment

2 a A – brain; B – spinal cord; C – nerves

b The brain and spinal cord

c i James's eyes and ears sense the potential danger.

ii Stimulus ➡ sense organ ➡ nerve ➡ brain or spinal cord ➡ muscle moving James out of danger ➡ response

Being in control

1 a The brain is protected by the skull.

b The brain controls (any two from): the blood pressure, breathing and heart rate.

c The human brain is able to (any two from): plan, control speech, reason and imagine.

d Neurones or nerves

e Boxing is dangerous because the boxer may be 'punch drunk' after a punch to the head and could possibly suffer brain damage.

What are we born with?

2 a A reflex action

b A – sensory neurone; B – spinal cord; C – motor neurone; D – muscle

c Part D (the muscle) is important because it contracts and pulls the body part away from danger.

d i Two from: coughing; blinking, sneezing.

ii Not including the brain in the reflex action speeds up the response.

e The frog has learnt that the food source will result in a painful sting. (This is called a learnt response.)

Learning behaviour in animals

2 a Train – to instruct
Obey – to do what you are told
Motivate – to provide an incentive
Behaviour – to respond to a stimulus

b Positive reinforcement

c Instead of offering food, the trainer could praise or show affection towards the dog.

d Roll the ball a very short distance in front of you and if the dog steps towards it use positive reinforcement to praise the dog (for example, saying 'good dog', using a food treat occasionally). Repeat the exercise until the dog realises that it will be rewarded for completing the action.

e Any two from: shouting, saying 'no', pushing the dog away, smacking.

f Puppies can learn hunting and feeding skills, defensive skills and body language for submission and aggression from their parents.

Aggression

1 a The F.A. is hoping that the initiative will reduce abusive language, aggressive behaviour and gang behaviour by creating a more relaxed 'family atmosphere'.

b Crowds show aggressive behaviour through: physical violence (hitting, throwing objects etc.) and taunting opposing team supporters (by teasing, singing and chanting rude comments about the players and supporters).

c Alcohol is related to an increase in aggression between supporters.

d In the wild a single animal may not behave in an aggressive fashion; however, when in a pack aggressive behaviour may increase. This is mimicked by humans, as in the case of behaviour at a football match.

How do I learn?

2 a Stimulation of the brain ➡ **Changes in the nerve cell** ➡ **Repetition** ➡ **Nerve pathway created** ➡ **Short-term memory created** ➡ Further repetition ➡ **Nerve pathway permanent** ➡ Long-term memory established

b Long-term memory is affected in the early stages of dementia.

c Teachers do not encourage students to carry out copying exercises because the activity does not encourage students to be involved in learning or to develop a memory of their learning. This means that they will not be able to learn effectively.

Effective learning

2 a 1 – Short term, 2 – Memory, 3 – Long term, 4 – Passive, 5 – Auditory, 6 – Kinaesthetic, 7 – Visual, 8 – Passive, 9 – Auditory

b Activities include (any four from): science practicals; following instructions; demonstration of an experiment; watching and taking notes from a video; reading; listening.

c Students to produce own mind map. The visual mind map should illustrate the nerves, motor nerve, sense organ, spinal cord and/or brain and muscle.

Topic 2 - Variation

Why are we different?

2 a Eye colour and height

b Skills, including swimming and netball

c A mixture of inherited and environmental factors. She may have inherited certain physical traits (such as height) that help her to play netball; but she can also improve her netball skills through training and practice. Her ability may also be affected by access to facilities.

d Jack will not be a good basketball player unless he has practised and trained in the skills of the game because basketball skills aren't inherited. However, he may have inherited some physical traits that would help him in the game.

e Genetic variation means that humans can adapt to changes in the environment. This allows them to survive outbreaks of disease.

How tall is this group?

2 a

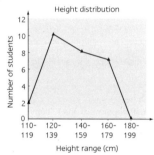

Height distribution

b 120–139 cm

c The sample taken by the Year 9 students may have been too small and the selected height range too large to produce an accurate picture of height in Year 9 students across the nation.

d Reducing the height range increments from 20 cm to 10 cm and carrying out repeat investigations on students of the same age.

e Other methods of measuring variation between Year 9 students may include: measuring the differences in the length of the little finger, the measurement of hand span, or a survey of eye colour.

What can twins tell us?

1 a They cannot be identical because they are not the same sex. Identical twins inherit the same genetic information and so are the same gender and have the same features (such as eye colour and shape of nose).

b i Out of the options listed, it is most likely that hair colour would be different.

ii Hair colour can be most easily changed. However, with the development of plastic surgery it is possible to change all physical features and even gender!

c They would have been brought up in different environments under different conditions. This could lead to changes in physical features such as build and height and in personality.

It came from my parents

1 a Nucleus – Structure located in a cell that contains chromosomes

Genes – Carry genetic information

Sperm – Male sex cell

Fertilisation – Fusion of male and female sex cells

Sex cells – Carry one set of genes from each parent

Cheek cell – Carries two sets of genes

b The testes produce the male sex cell; the ovaries produce the female sex cell.

c i A sperm cell – 23 chromosomes

ii An egg cell – 23 chromosomes

iii A fertilised egg cell – 46 chromosomes

iv A nerve cell – 46 chromosomes

d A baby has characteristics from both parents because it has inherited genetic information from the sex cells of both parents, including hair colour, eye colour, other facial features, build and height.

Natural clones

3 a Egg cell taken from sheep A ➔ **Nucleus of cell removed** ➔ Cells taken from the udder of sheep B ➔ **Nucleus removed** ➔ **Nucleus from sheep B placed into egg cell of sheep A** ➔ Egg cell transplanted into female sheep to grow ➔ Clone of sheep B born

b The cutting looks the same because it has the same genetic information as the parent plant.

c The fruit and vegetables are of the same quality, taste, shape and colour.

d Cloning leads to a lack of variation in the offspring and a reduction in the gene pool.

e Production is quick and relatively cheap with more offspring being produced.

f There are ethical concerns regarding cloning due to the high death rate and early death of the cloned animals.

Dog breeding

2 a The wolf

b i Artificial or selective breeding

ii The disadvantages are that it can take several generations to breed out unwanted features, while potential health problems are bred in.

c Any three from: hunting, dogs for the blind, herding animals, sniffer dogs, petting dogs (and any other sensible answer).

d Dogs can be bred with the features that they need for specific roles such as a good sense of smell for hunting and long limbs for racing (and any other sensible choices).

e In line breeding, distant relatives with desirable features are bred together. Only the dogs from their offspring with the new desirable features are selected for further breeding.

Topic 3 - Chemical patterns

The alkali metals

2 a Lithium, **sodium,** potassium and rubidium are the first four elements in **Group 1,** the **alkali** metals. The first **three** of these metals are **less** dense than water and float on the surface. They are **silvery** when cut but tarnish when in air. Lithium is the **least** reactive and rubidium is the **most** reactive of the four. All four metals have **similar** properties.

b i Metal A – lithium; Metal B – potassium; Metal C – sodium

ii (Least reactive)

A Lithium

B Sodium

C Potassium

c Caesium and francium

Word and symbol equations

2 a A chemical **reaction** takes place between **two** or more **reactants,** combining together to form one or more **new** and **different** substances (the **products** of the reaction).

b The reactants are sodium and water.

The products are sodium hydroxide and hydrogen

c i Sodium + oxygen ➔ **sodium oxide**

ii The reactants are sodium and oxygen. The new compound is sodium oxide.

Reacting metals

3 a Hydrogen

b You would test the gas in Experiment A by placing the opening of the test tube near a lighted splint. If hydrogen is present the gas should 'pop'.

c The litmus solution would turn blue.

d Calcium hydroxide

e If the lighted splint is placed near the exit delivery tube in Experiment B a flame would be observed as the hydrogen gas burned.

f Experiment A – $Ca + 2H_2O ➔ Ca(OH)_2 + H_2$

Experiment B – $Mg + H_2O ➔ MgO + H_2$

Metals and acids

2 a

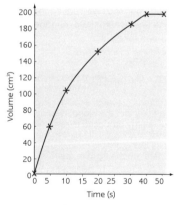

b 80 cm³

c After 40 seconds the reaction halts.

d i

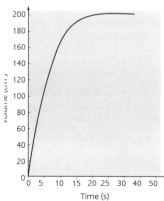

ii Calcium

e magnesium + hydrochloric acid ➡ magnesium chloride + hydrogen

Acid concentration

3 a i magnesium + hydrochloric acid ➡ magnesium chloride + hydrogen

ii $Mg + 2HCl$ ➡ $MgCl_2 + H_2$

b Acid X is most concentrated.

c The rate of reaction is greater at A.

d The higher the acid concentration, the faster the reaction (or the reverse).

e The graph levels off because the reaction slows down and stops as the reactants are used up.

Displacement of metals

2 a Magnesium

b There would be no reaction because copper cannot displace zinc.

c iron + copper sulphate ➡ iron sulphate + copper

d The iron would become coated in copper.

e (From least reactive) copper ➡ iron ➡ zinc ➡ metal X (magnesium)

Predicting reactions

2 a Silver is located above gold.

b Carbon is located above iron in the reactivity series and can therefore displace the iron from the oxide ore.

c Zinc and tin could also be displaced.

d It is possible because zinc is more reactive than iron – it reacts with air to produce a protective layer for the steel below which would normally rust.

Corrosion of metals

1 a Gold – Used to manufacture electrical connections in computers

Titanium – Used in replacement body parts

Stainless steel – Used for surfaces in hospital operating theatres

Aluminium – Used for making cooking foil

Platinum – Used to make jewellery

Chromium and nickel – Used in stainless steel to manufacture cutlery

b Gold and platinum do not react with air and therefore do not tarnish.

c To prevent corrosion and therefore reduce the hazard of contamination to food.

d Two from: lead, copper, zinc

e Steel is abundant and therefore cheap, whereas aluminium is expensive to extract from its ore.

How to stop corrosion

1 a When vehicles become rusty, they become weaker and less able to withstand an impact in an accident.

b i The nail will rust in test tube A

ii The iron nail will not rust in the other test tubes because:

Test tube B – there is no oxygen in the water.

Test tube C – the layer of paint protects the iron nail from oxygen and water.

Test tube D – water is removed from the air.

iii Water and oxygen are needed for rusting.

iv A test tube open to the air containing an untreated iron nail could act as a control.

v The zinc coating on the nail keeps out the water and oxygen.

Topic 4 – Chemical reactions

Metals and non-metals

1 a A, E

b They are all magnetic metals.

c Tungsten is similar to other metals because most metals have a high melting point.

d Carbon is unusual because it is a non-metal and it conducts electricity.

e Graphite is a suitable material for pencils because its structure is in layers that are soft and slippery and transfer themselves to the paper when we write.

Acids, alkalis and bases

2 a Soluble bases are called alkalis.

b i sulphuric acid + sodium hydroxide ➡ **sodium sulphate** + **water**

ii pH7

c sulphuric acid + potassium hydroxide ➡ potassium sulphate + water

Carbonates and acids

1 a i Carbon dioxide   ii Limewater

iii The limewater turns cloudy.

b There would be no colour change in the blue litmus paper.

c No colour change indicates that the acid has been destroyed (neutralised).

Salts

2 a i Neutralisation of an **acid** by a base produces a salt:

acid + base ➡ a salt + water. In this reaction the **hydrogen** in the acid is replaced with a **metal**, as in the example with **sodium** chloride.

ii Hydrochloric acid + sodium hydroxide ➡ **sodium chloride** + **water**

b We use the salt for seasoning food or lowering the melting point of road ice (in order to melt dangerous ice on the roads).

c Sulphate salts are produced during reactions with sulphuric acid.

d Through evaporation

Making a salt

3 a Hydrochloric acid produces **chloride** salts. Sulphuric acid produces **sulphate** salts. Nitric acid produces **nitrate** salts.

b i Hydrochloric acid + sodium hydroxide ➡ sodium chloride + water

$HCl + NaOH$ ➡ $NaCl + H_2O$

ii This type of reaction is called a neutralisation reaction.

iii Evaporation is used to remove the water.

c i Example of a reaction between an acid and insoluble base:

copper oxide + sulphuric acid ➡ copper sulphate + water

$CuO + H_2SO_4$ ➡ $CuSO_4 + H_2O$

Note: other correct examples also acceptable.

ii Example of a reaction between an acid and a metal:

zinc oxide + sulphuric acid ➡ zinc sulphate + water

$ZnO + H_2SO_4$ ➡ $ZnSO_4 + H_2O$

Note: other correct examples also acceptable.

d i Sodium nitrate, copper nitrate

ii Calcium sulphate

iii Potassium chloride, hydrochloric acid Or any other sensible example.

Precipitating salts

1 a The rate of reaction is greatest at B.

b As the temperature increases, the rate of reaction increases.

c You would make it a fair test by using the same concentration and volume of acid at each temperature.

d The rate at which precipitate is produced would increase and rise more quickly.

Using salts

2 a Dissolving the salt in water, filtering out the sand and then evaporating the water away.

b Filtration will not remove the soluble pink impurities.

c Potassium chloride (KCl)

d By filtration

Topic 5 – Pressure, forces and moments

Pressure points

3 a A: $p = f/a = 40\,N/80\,cm^2 = 0.5\,N/cm^2$
B: $10\,N/25\,cm^2 = 0.4\,N/cm^2$
Block B exerts the least pressure.

b $f = p \times a$
$20\,N/mm^2 \times 2\,mm^2 = 40\,N$

c The stiletto heel will place a concentrated force on a small area. This leads to a high pressure and indents in the floor.

d $p = f/a = 20\,N/0.2\,mm^2 = 100\,000\,000\,N/m^2$ or $1 \times 10^8\,N/m^2$

e $a = f/p = 600\,N/240\,N/m^2 = 2.5\,m^2$
width = area/length = $2.5/2 = 1.25\,m$

Pressure in gases

2 a Air particles colliding with the sides of the balloon is the force responsible for causing the pressure inside the balloon.

b i The air particles will move closer together.

ii The pressure inside the balloon will increase. This is because the air particles will be closer together and therefore collide more often.

c The pressure inside the balloon can also be increased by blowing more air into the balloon and by warming the balloon.

Pressure in liquids

1 a Pressure increases with depth, so the dam wall must be stronger as depth increases to withstand the pressure of the water.

b Scuba divers must not dive too deep because the pressure of the water on their bodies can be dangerously high at increased depth while the pressure within their bodies remains the same.

c i

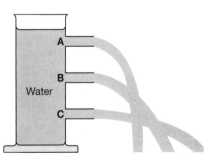

ii Water travels furthest from spout C.

iii Pressure increases with depth, forcing the water to travel further.

d The distance between the water particles will remain the same because liquids cannot be compressed.

e i That pressure acts in all directions.

ii We could see that the water pours out from the holes equally, showing that pressure in water is the same at any one depth.

Turning forces and moments

3 a The sliding weight must be moved further away from the pivot to balance the crane.

b The turning moment is: 3 N × 0.4 m = 1.2 Nm

c Newton metres (Nm)

d Force × 0.1 m = 3 N × 0.4 m

So the weight of the toy car is 12 N

e The wide base makes the wine glass more stable because a larger moment would be needed to overcome the weight of the glass and knock it over.

The Body Machine

2 a The biceps

b

c

d The triceps

e Antagonistic pairs

Speedy sums

1 a Speed = $\frac{distance}{time}$ = $\frac{200}{5}$ = 40 m/s

b If the car is travelling at a steady speed the forces will be balanced.

c Distance = speed × time = 2 × 3 = 6 miles

d The speed of the hill walker is called the 'average speed' because the walker's speed will vary (at times walking quicker than 2 mph and at times slower) and the journey will also include periods of rest. This means that the walker will not be consistently walking at 2 mph.

Distance–time graphs

2 a A – Cycling along a level road

B – Stops for lunch

C – Riding uphill

D – Riding downhill

b

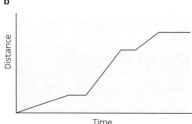

Topic 6 – Energy transfers

Sources of light

1 a The creation of **shadows** relies upon the fact that light travels in **straight lines** and that light cannot travel through **opaque** materials, but only through materials that are **transparent**. Our Sun is a **luminous** star. Stars, fires and lamps all **emit** light.

b i

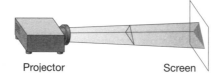

Projector   Screen

ii To make the shadow smaller you could move the opaque object further away from the light source or move the projector further away from the opaque object.

iii Students' diagrams should show the object is moved closer to the light source.

Light and plane mirrors

2 a

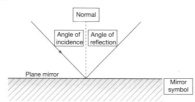

b The properties of the image are (any three from): it is as far behind the mirror as the object is in front; it is the same size as the object; it is virtual; it is laterally inverted.

c

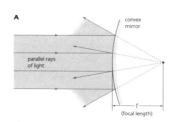

d Student's diagram should show the image located the same distance behind the mirror as the object is in front.

e It is called a virtual image.

Curved mirrors

2 a A – convex mirror; B – concave mirror.

b

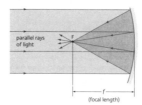

c The images formed by a convex mirror are virtual and upright.

d A concave mirror is used by shavers because it forms an image that is both upright and magnified.

e Concave mirrors are called 'converging mirrors' because they converge the rays of light, bringing them to a focus.

f Car wing mirrors are convex because the convex mirror provides a wider field of view and produces an image that is upright (although the image is smaller).

Total internal reflection

3 a

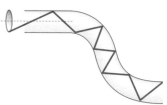

b An optical cable is a cable made up from hundreds and thousands of optical fibres that can be used to transmit light signals over long distances.

c In an endoscope one set of fibres will be used to illuminate the object being viewed and the second set will transmit the image back to the user.

d Endoscopes are used in engineering, for example for viewing inaccessible parts of a structure such as an aeroplane wing, or to look for cracks. (Any other sensible answer acceptable also.)

e Optical cables can carry more information, are less expensive and lighter than copper cables.

Refraction

2 a

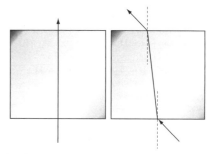

b Refraction

c When a ray of light enters denser transparent material it bends **towards** the normal because the light is **slowed down**.

d

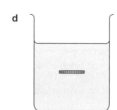

The coin will appear closer to the surface of the water, as shown here

Isaac Newton 'the optickian'

2 a i

   ii Red light

   iii Violet light

   iv Red light

b Light is refracted by different amounts as each colour light has a different wavelength.

c The phenomenon of splitting white light into its component colours is called 'dispersion'.

Colour

2 a i A white object is seen as white in white light because it reflects all seven colours of the spectrum and absorbs none.

   ii A red object is seen as red in white light because only the red light is reflected.

b Red light will pass through the red filter and blue light will pass through the blue filter.

c i Black

   ii White light will be dispersed into the visible spectrum. Only green light will pass through the green filter, but the green light will be absorbed by the red object. The red object will therefore appear black.

Using colour

2 a The three primary colours of light are red, green and blue.

b

Adding blue and red makes magenta (purple)

Adding blue and green makes cyan (light blue)

Adding red and green makes yellow

Adding all three makes white again

c White light can be seen in the centre of the colours in answer **b**.

d i The red shoes appear red in white light because the red component in the white light is reflected while all of the other colours are absorbed.

   ii The red shoes will appear black in blue light because the blue light is absorbed.

Seeing the light

2 a

b **A** – iris, **B** – cornea, **C** – lens, **D** – pupil, **E** – optic nerve, **F** – retina

c i Iris

   ii Lens

d Retina

e The role of the optic nerve is to carry nervous impulses from the eye to the brain.

Resistance in circuits

3 a i The independent variable is the length of the wire.

   ii The dependent variable is resistance.

b i

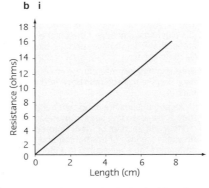

   ii If the length of wire doubles, the resistance also doubles.

c Nichrome wire has a higher resistance than a length of copper wire of the same dimensions.

Modelling circuits

3 a i

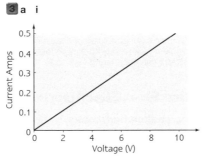

   ii As the voltage increases, the current also increases.

   iii When the voltage doubles, the current also doubles.

b 0.8 A

c The current readings would decrease.

d Precautions must be taken against touching the wire because it will become hot. This is because at high resistances a lot of energy is transferred as heat to the wire.

e Resistance = voltage/current = 12/4 = $3\,\Omega$ (Ohms)

Using electricity

a i

Appliance	Useful energy	Wasted energy
Light bulb	Light	Heat
Electric heater	Heat	Light
Electric hairdryer	Heat	Sound
Electric drill	Kinetic	Sound
Electric toaster	Heat	Light

   ii

Appliance	Alternative method
Light bulb	Candle
Electric heater	Coal or wood fire
Electric hairdryer	Combing and fresh air
Electric drill	Hand drill
Electric toaster	Wood fire

b Low-energy light bulbs reduce the electrical energy consumed.

c The advantages of using electricity include (any four from): it is easily transferred from place to place in electric cables; it can be obtained from batteries that are mobile; it can be transported over long distances; it can be switched on and off rapidly; the energy output from electrical circuits can easily be controlled; electrical energy can be converted into a large variety of other forms of energy including light, heat and kinetic energy.

Electricity in the home

1 a The electric heater converts electrical energy into **heat** energy. The amount of energy the heater uses per **second** is called its 'power'. Power is measured in **watts**.

b **A** Low-energy light bulb

   E Light bulb

   D Kettle

   C Washing machine

   B Electric cooker

c The government wishes householders to replace their traditional bulbs with low-energy bulbs because the low-energy bulbs use less power and so consume less energy. Therefore, they conserve resources.

d 1500 J/2500 J x 100% = 60%

Topic 7 – Humans and the environment

What resources do we need?

1 a Deforestation is mainly carried out to provide land (that can be used to grow crops) for a growing population.

b The areas of deforestation have increased because there is increasing demand for resources as the population increases.

c Deforestation leads to (two from): soil erosion; poor fertility of the remaining land (the result of the soil erosion); pollution in the form of rubbish, gas emissions or industrial waste, if the land is developed.

d i Pesticides – chemicals used to destroy insect pests that feed on the crops.

    Fertilisers – provide minerals needed for plant growth.

   ii The fertilisers and pesticides are washed off the farm land and flow into the rivers, polluting drinking water.

The effect of acid on plants

2 a i Tap water averages: length of shoot 48.8 mm; length of root 24.8 mm

    Acid rain water averages: length of shoot 39.8 mm; length of root 16.5 mm

   ii

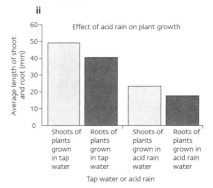

b Difference in shoot length: 48.8 – 39.8 = 9 mm

   Difference in root length: 24.8 – 16.5 = 8.3 mm

c Carbon dioxide and sulphur dioxide (and oxides of nitrogen)

d The crops grown in regions of acid rain will be of poor quality – root growth will be poor and shoots will be stunted.

e In order to evaluate your evidence you would compare your two sets of results and then compare these with other studies carried out on different plants.

How clean is our air?

1 **a** The leaves and bark of the trees were coated in soot.

b There were many factories and heavy industries during the Industrial Revolution and these burnt large quantities of fuels. Burning fuels produces soot. Coal in particular produces high levels of soot when burnt and this was widely used in industry during the Industrial Revolution. Soot takes the form of fine particles.

c The moths' dark colouring gave them camouflage which meant that they could stay hidden from predatory birds.

d The air in Britain today is less polluted with soot and so the trees are not coated in soot. This means that the lighter-coloured moth is now better camouflaged against the tree bark than the darker moth.

What happened to the atmosphere?

3 **a** Carbon dioxide, methane, nitrogen oxides

b Carbon dioxide and nitrogen oxide are produced by the combustion of fossil fuels. Methane is a product of digestion in cows and is also produced by bacteria (for example, in rice paddy fields).

c Greenhouse gases trap heat as it is reflected from the Earth's surface, preventing it from leaving Earth and causing an increase in temperature – global warming.

d Infra-red radiation passes through the atmosphere. Some of the infra-red radiation is absorbed by the greenhouse gases in the atmosphere, trapping the heat. The heat is radiated in all directions by the surface of the Earth and clouds. This warms the Earth and atmosphere.

e City centres are heat spots and so may artificially raise the temperature of readings taken.

f Increases in CFC gases have led to the depletion of the ozone layer. This depletion allows ultraviolet (UV) rays to pass to the Earth, increasing the possibility of skin cancer and damage to plants.

Looking at your surroundings

2 **a**

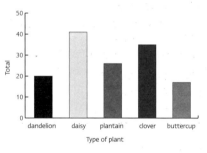

b $1 \, m^2 \times 10$ quadrats $= 10 \, m^2$

c The daisy

d The area sampled is small in comparison with the whole area of the verge. It is only representative of the whole verge.

e The area sampled was $10 \, m^2$. $1000 \, m^2$ is 100 times the area of the sample. There are 17 buttercups in $10 \, m^2$, so in $1000 \, m^2$ there are $17 \times 100 = 1700$ buttercups.

Conservation

1 **a** The osprey is so closely protected because it is close to extinction. If the eggs are stolen they will not hatch and the bird may become extinct.

b Breeding programmes can be set up, releasing the red squirrels back into the habitat.

c Trees and bushes are important habitats – they act as breeding sites, places for nesting and sources of food. Deforestation results in the loss of this habitat and endangers the species that live there.

d The animals can be captured and relocated to a safe area.

Can we save the planet?

1 **a** Plane travel

b $\dfrac{2.6}{2.6} = 1$ year

c $\dfrac{2.6}{0.8} = 3.25$ flights $= 4$ flights to Spain.

d Car owners can reduce the carbon emissions from their cars by: travelling less; improving their driving methods (such as driving in a suitable gear); maintaining the vehicle regularly; buying a more fuel-efficient car; car sharing.

Topic 8 – Geology

Studying sedimentary rocks

1 **a** Sandstone

b Sedimentary rock

c The rock is made from grains of sand.

d The particles are held together by natural cements such as calcite or silica.

e The term used for the laying down of new layers of rock is deposition.

f Any two from: erosion by the wind, erosion by water, expansion of ice within the rock, chemical attack.

More about sediments

1 **a** Large swampy forests were located in these areas. (Coal is formed from plant remains in swamps.)

b **i** It suggests that the climate must have been temperate enough (or even tropical) for fern plants to survive.

ii The trees and plants fell into the muddy swamp and this prevented the air from reaching the plants. As a result the plants did not rot away.

c **i** Coal is called a 'fossil fuel' because fossils are found in it.

ii Other fossil fuels are crude oil and natural gas.

d Coal can be identified as a sedimentary rock because it is made up of layers and contains evidence of fossils.

Mountains and folds

2 **a** An earthquake or tectonic plate movements resulting in huge forces could be responsible for causing the fault.

b Layer D

c It suggests that the cliff face was once under water but it has risen up and out of the sea.

d The weight of the cliff face creates great pressure on the lower strata, causing compression in the bottom layers of rock.

Metamorphic rocks

3 **a** Marble

b Limestone

c The limestone has been heated by the hot magma, baking it.

d Quartzite is formed from quartz crystals, making the rock highly resistant to weathering and very hard.

e Metamorphic rocks can be formed at all tectonic plate boundaries where the conditions of high pressure and temperature exist.

Crystals in igneous rocks

2 **a** The crystals in the pillow basalt will be small.

b Quartz crystals were formed by cooling slowly above the ground.

c The crystals were formed under great pressure.

d The heat that forms the metamorphic rock destroys the fossils.

e All of the crystals in the different rocks have straight edges and sharp corners. This will be reflected in the student's drawing.

Volcanic magic

3 **a** One plate dips below the other because it has a greater density.

b Friction creates heat between the two plates, causing the rock to melt and forming magma.

c Magma accumulates in chambers until the pressure builds up and the magma forces its way through cracks in the Earth's crust. This forms the volcanic eruption.

d Increased pressure in the chamber of the volcano causes the volcano to erupt.

e The magma contains material from both plates, sea water and sediments from the sea.

The rock cycle

2 **a** metamorphic rocks ➡ weathering ➡ erosion ➡ transport ➡ deposition ➡ sediments ➡ sedimentary rocks

b Magma is formed from melting rocks and is released onto the surface of the Earth by volcanoes.

c Small crystals

d During transportation the rocks will be broken down in size and become rounded.

e A sedimentary rock can be 'second-hand' because it can change its form. It may be changed into a metamorphic rock by increases in pressure and heat; then melt to form magma within a volcano; then become an igneous rock; and finally, following weathering, return once again to its form as a sedimentary rock.